Achieving National Board Certification
for
School Library Media Specialists

A *Study Guide*

GAIL DICKINSON

D1235618

AMERICAN LIBRARY ASSOCIATION
Chicago   2006

"National Board for Professional Teaching Standards," "NBPTS" "National Board Certification," and "National Board Certified Teacher" are registered trademarks and are used with permission from the National Board for Professional Teaching Standards. All rights reserved. For more information about National Board Certification, visit http://www.nbpts.org.

Printed on 50-pound white offset paper, a pH-neutral stock, and bound in 10-point cover stock by Victor Graphics.

The paper used in this publication meets the minimum requirements of American National Standard for Information Sciences—Permanence of Paper for Printed Library Materials, ANSI Z39.48-1992. ∞

Library of Congress Cataloging-in-Publication Data

Dickinson, Gail K.
    Achieving national board certification for school library media specialists : a study guide / Gail Dickinson.
       p. cm.
    Includes bibliographical references and index.
    ISBN 0-8389-0901-9
    1. School librarians—Certification—Standards—United States. 2. Instructional materials personnel—Certification—Standards—United States. 3. Media programs (Education)—United States. I. Title.

    Z682.4.S34D53 2005
    027.8—dc22   2005018844

Printed in the United States of America

10 09 08 07 06   5 4 3 2 1

To my sisters—Gretta, Brenda, Susan, and Beth—who, like all sisters, create their own standards for assessments in life. Friends come and go, but sisters are forever.

Contents

Figures

Acknowledgments

I gratefully acknowledge the patience and assistance of my editor, Laura Pelehach, for her constant encouragement. The National Board for Professional Teaching Standards has graciously given me permission to use materials on its website in order to encourage school library media candidates. Ann Marie Pipkin gave thoughtful and constructive comments on the manuscript, which were invaluable. I also acknowledge the leadership, courage, and fortitude of the now almost 1,200 National Board Certified Teachers in school library media. You are blazing the trail for others to follow and are an inspiration to the profession.

Introduction

The process developed by the National Board for Professional Teaching Standards (NBPTS) for becoming a National Board Certified Teacher (NBCT) has been described as rigorous, intense, fulfilling, and as the best professional growth experience one could ever have. In other words, it's scary. My introduction to NBPTS was in a packed ballroom at a North Carolina School Library Media Association conference in fall 2000. In this room filled with skilled, confident, and experienced school library media specialists, the fear was palpable. My thought as I watched the anxiety level was that the profession needed to join together to provide help to the building-level practitioner facing this challenge.

This book will not reduce the workload involved in attempting to achieve National Board certification. In fact, it may increase it. It won't make the process any easier, but it won't make it any harder either. What is intended by this book is to make the process less scary. Any mountain appears to be unscalable at first glance. A closer and more careful look reveals the ledges, handholds, and indentations that make the climb possible.

The National Board certification process is a test of one's teaching knowledge and skill, and specifically of teaching skills in the area of school library media. It is also a writing test, a test of organizational ability, and a test of patience and stamina. The teaching skills, experience, and knowledge of school library media are what a prospective candidate brings to the process. This book provides some avenues to strengthen and enhance those knowledge and skills based on my knowledge of the school library field, my experience in teaching school library media, and my time spent listening to the voices of school library media NBCTs and candidates.

This book is not intended to be a quick fix, and it will not guarantee success. It is input into the process. The more you know, the more you can plot your own path to success. NBPTS is one way, and perhaps the only way, that we school library media specialists can be judged by the same criteria as our classroom teaching peers. We try so hard as a field for equal recognition. A National Board Certified Teacher is the leader in that field. We need as many school library media NBCTs as possible in order to stand as equals to accomplished teachers in all fields. The two documents that you will need at your side as you begin this process are the "NBPTS Library Media Standards," which is available through NBPTS; and *Information Power*, which contains the national standards for the school library profession. The certification process is based on interwoven threads of these two sets of powerful standards. Before the process is finished, you may be able to recite large chunks of each by heart.

This book is divided into three parts. The first is a history and overview of NBPTS and the certification process. Part 2 reviews the knowledge base of the pieces of the school library media field that are especially highlighted in the NBPTS portfolio entries and assessment center exercises. Part 3 pulls apart the portfolio entries and assessment center exercises, and gives tips on how to complete those pieces. Part 3 also discusses what to do if you do not achieve NBCT status the first time, and explores the concept of life as an NBCT, and how the NBPTS process could change our profession.

This book is intended primarily for school library media specialists who are deciding whether or not to attempt the certification process, and for those who have made that decision and are planning their candidacy. It will also be helpful for NBPTS registered candidate supporters, and for school library media educators who are looking for ways to incorporate NBPTS skills into school library media preparation programs. It has also been suggested that this book may be of value to those who simply want to become better at what they do.

The building-level school library media specialist is the only person who can become a school library media NBCT. Those of us on the sidelines—the supervisors, professors, researchers, writers, and others in the school library media community—can only watch and cheer as the race is run. This book is one attempt at smoothing the path. The energy that is put into the race is up to you.

PART I *Overview*

This part, comprising the first four chapters, is a history and overview of the National Board for Professional Teaching Standards and its certification process. In order to understand the NBPTS process, one must first understand how NBPTS came to be, and what it is trying to achieve in the field of education. NBPTS is based on teaching expertise and on educational best practices.

It seems at times that all professions compare themselves to medicine as the one true profession. The fact that NBPTS is historically based on changes in medical education will not be a surprise, and may provide some insight into library science education as well.

It is suggested that the candidate refer to this part when reading the school library media standards. A thorough understanding of NBPTS, its core principles, and its school library media standards is necessary before beginning the certification process. Read, think, and reflect.

1 National Board History and Overview

ORIGINS

It all started with *A Nation at Risk*. In 1983 the National Commission on Excellence in Education released its report, *A Nation at Risk: The Imperative for Educational Reform*. Found in this report are the infamous words: "If an unfriendly foreign power had attempted to impose on America the mediocre educational performance that exists today, we might well have viewed it as an act of war."[1] These words were the basis for an educational revolution. Shock waves rolled through the educational bureaucratic structure. Reform efforts arose, were implemented, and faded almost overnight.

Other changes were longer-lasting. Reforms in school structure such as year-round schooling and block scheduling attempted to address the issues of creating larger blocks of time for instruction and changing the rote lecture, drill, and practice of teaching. Other changes targeted school organization. Site-based management and decentralization of authority, as examples of organizational changes, were enacted to delegate decision-making power to teachers and school staff, rather than authority being maintained at the district level. The desire to individualize the school experience on the local level was mitigated, though, by changes in curriculum, including an increase in standardized testing and the push for a national curriculum.

3

A Nation at Risk became the touchstone for educational reforms on a wide scale. Other educational foundations and associations generated reports that focused on this document, either as responses to the criticisms outlined in *A Nation at Risk* or in support of planned changes. To the dismay of the library field, the importance of libraries to the educational process was mentioned only slightly in most of these reports, and school libraries, long posited as the hub of the school, were not mentioned at all. This was especially dismaying because the 1986 edition of *Information Power* was in the process of being developed, and many of the changes in its new guidelines for school library programs incorporated the types of reforms that were being called for.[2] These omissions sparked immediate action on the part of the library communities. Their responses were gathered and published in a collection of papers entitled *Libraries and the Learning Society*.[3] The response written by the American Association of School Librarians (AASL), for example, focused on the areas described in *A Nation at Risk* with which the school library media profession had special concern and highlighted the "unique contributions that [school library media specialists] make in the implementation of these recommendations."[4]

Another response to *A Nation at Risk* that generated almost as much attention as the original was prepared by the Carnegie Task Force on Teaching as a Profession. *A Nation Prepared: Teachers for the 21st Century* (1986) examined the preparation and retention of teachers and posited a new model for teacher education.[5] The model, as with many changes in education, was based on the medical profession. A past Carnegie study on medicine in 1910 had produced the Flexner Report, which changed the practice of medicine and the teaching and preparation of physicians.[6] The Flexner Report called for a restructuring of the preparation of the medical education professoriat and proposed high national standards for the medical profession, with a degree of self-regulation.

Specifically, the report noted that a sound medical education comprises three factors. First and foremost is an understanding of the knowledge base, referred to as the "fundamental sciences underlying the study of medicine." Second, the training of doctors should incorporate the investigation of new knowledge along with the study of existing knowledge. Instructors engaged in preparing new professionals for the medical field should be directly involved with these investigations, so that new medical professionals could understand how new knowledge is created, tested, and incorporated into existing medical practices. And third, the knowledge base and investigation should include direct supervised practice, specifically in a teaching hospital under the control of the medical school. With some minor revisions over time, those changes are still in effect today in the education of doctors.

In schools of education, this model of knowledge base, integrated theory and practice, and the concept of professional development schools working with universities has now become the norm as well. These changes can be traced back directly to *A Nation Prepared* in the same way that changes in preparation for the medical profession can be traced back to the Flexner Report.

A Nation Prepared analyzed the teaching profession within the framework of *A Nation at Risk*. It found the problem was not that good teachers did not exist, or that colleges and universities were not preparing the best teachers that they could, although suggestions were made for improvement. The major problem had more to do with the structure of the teaching profession. New teachers arrived at schools to begin their career and were paid at basically the same level as all new teachers, regardless of differing quality in their teacher training. The best new teachers were not offered any more money than mediocre new teachers. The level of skill might be a hiring preference, but once inside the classroom door, good teachers were paid no more than not-so-good teachers. Salary increases tended to be awarded according to seniority and experience, with some differential for additional education such as master's degrees.

After ten years of teaching, mediocre teachers and excellent teachers were still paid exactly the same salary. The only way for a teacher to make more money and still remain a classroom teacher was to work longer hours, by coaching, tutoring, or teaching summer school. The bureaucratic structure of schools also provided little career advancement for teachers. Despite the desire of some innovative districts to create master teachers, teacher leaders, or other ways to provide career ladders, the daily life of teachers remained the same for their entire career. Skill and experience might improve one's level of confidence, but for a classroom teacher Day 1,576 would unfold in roughly the same way as did Day 1.

The Carnegie Task Force investigated the reasons that good teachers left teaching, and grouped these in several categories. First, it found that teachers wanted to make more money. Teachers could leave the profession of education to work in the private sector for substantially more money than they could make as teachers. If teachers stayed in education, their only way to increase their income, other than moonlighting or second jobs, was to accept positions in administration at the building level or the central office. These positions tended to be limited in number, with one principal and several assistant principals serving a building with 100 or more teachers. This also meant that good teachers who moved into administrative positions, even if they became good administrators, were no longer teaching students in classrooms. So regardless of whether good teachers went into private industry or moved up through the teaching ranks to become department chairs, school principals, or central office personnel, they still were no longer teaching the nation's students.

The task force's assessment of the teaching profession centered on one problem: how to keep the nation's best teachers in the classroom. Its solutions centered on three issues listed simplistically below:

- Describe what great teaching is
- Identify great teachers
- Pay them more money

The task force outlined several strategies for improvement in the teaching profession, including the development of more rigorous hands-on preparation, increased mentoring for beginning teachers, and most importantly, the development of a national board for teaching standards.

THE FOUNDING OF THE NATIONAL BOARD

One of the most direct impacts of *A Nation Prepared* was in regard to the creation of a national board. The text in *A Nation Prepared* is as follows: "Create a National Board for Professional Teaching Standards, organized with a regional and state membership structure, to establish high standards for what teachers need to know and be able to do, and to certify teachers who meet that standard."[7]

The National Board for Professional Teaching Standards was created in 1987 with a three-part objective that is almost verbatim from the previous text. The mission and objectives of NBPTS are to advance the quality of teaching and learning by

maintaining high and rigorous standards for what accomplished teachers should know and be able to do;

providing a national voluntary system certifying teachers who meet these standards; and

advocating related education reforms to integrate National Board Certification in American education and to capitalize on the expertise of National Board Certified Teachers.[8]

By and large, the first two objectives have been achieved. The NBPTS process has developed high and rigorous standards, and provides teachers with a process to achieve National Board certification. With well over 40,000 teachers identified as accomplished, it cannot be denied that achieving National Board Certified Teacher status is seen as desirable by teachers.[9]

Changes in policy, however, have been less easy to achieve. There is little information found in the literature on the supervision or evaluation of NBCTs, or to surmise that the approach of the building administrator to working with an NBCT is any different from working with a non-NBCT. In other words, we really don't know if principals approach evaluating an accomplished teacher any differently than they would evaluating any other teacher. We also don't know if school district evaluation systems take any perceived difference between an NBCT and a non-NBCT into account by form, process, or ranking. The identification of accomplished teachers has tremendous potential impact on the perception of education as a profession. Exactly what those impacts might be on the perceptions of school administrators, the general public, or legislators is not yet known.

THE NATIONAL BOARD PROCESS

The voice of the classroom teacher has always been important to the National Board. More than half of the members of its founding Board of Directors were practicing classroom teachers, and each succeeding board has followed suit, mandating that over half of the membership be practicing classroom teachers. Each standards writing committee has also counted more than half of its membership as building-level practitioners in that subject area. The national standards and core propositions for what teachers should know and be able to do are teacher-developed and teacher-tested. Classroom teachers specifically trained as assessors by NBPTS score all entries and exercises in the certification process for each subject area.

Five Core Propositions

The five core propositions are the basis for the NBPTS standards, portfolio instructions, and assessments. (A full exploration of each proposition can be found at http://www.nbpts.org.) These propositions serve as the basis for what teachers should know and be able to do, and are the philosophical basis for subject standards. The standards for each teaching specialty weave these core propositions into subject area standards, portfolio entries, and assessment center exercises.

PROPOSITION ONE
Teachers Are Committed to Students and Their Learning

This proposition arguably is the basis for the teaching profession. It is assumed that prospective teachers have a special commitment to children that creates the desire to teach, and moves a young person to pursue a career in the education field. In response to the question of why he or she chose teaching as a profession, a teacher may respond, "because I like children." Although that statement is still an important indicator for teacher hiring, this proposition takes that feeling for children far beyond an emotional reaction or sentimental attachment. It presumes that good teachers have an intellectual understanding of learning theory, and that they can apply their understanding to the children they teach. Teachers treat children as individuals and care about their learning in a holistic sense.

Accomplished teachers recognize that learning happens both in and out of school. Teachers encourage the development of the whole child, with a sense of responsibility for the development of the child into the adult. Teachers understand the impact that the child's family, home, and community life have on learning, and take pains to be aware and involved in that life beyond school.

School library media specialists may respond to the question of why they chose this specialty by saying that they wanted to connect children to a love of reading. In the same way as teachers, accomplished library media specialists turn the "because I like books" answer into a deeper understanding of children and their communities, as well as a deeper understanding of the world of information.

PROPOSITION TWO
Teachers Know the Subjects They Teach
and How to Teach Those Subjects to Students

A knowledge of learning theory is important, but not enough. Teachers have to be subject experts first, and then be expert teachers in that subject. Teaching language arts takes different knowledge, skills, and abilities than does teaching math. For school library media specialists, this means that their expertise must be gained in the general areas of library and information science and also in the specific areas of information skills, literature in all formats, and in technology. Special attention in school library media education must then be given to teaching those subjects to children. For example, professionals in the school library media field must know quality children's literature, and they must also know how to apply theories of motivation to encourage children to read. They must understand technology and be able to teach the use of technology as a tool in the context of information skills.

PROPOSITION THREE
Teachers Are Responsible for Managing
and Monitoring Student Learning

Managing and monitoring student learning includes the traditional teaching skills of classroom management and discipline, but it also goes beyond these to include the entire learning process. Teachers are aware of how student learning styles affect the learning process, and they modify their instruction to maximize learning for each student. Teachers track student learning through a variety of formal and informal assessment methods, and they modify their instruction based on their analysis of the assessment results. As will be seen later, this standard presents more of a challenge to school library media specialists than to other teachers. Although skilled in the practices designed to create information-literate users and lifelong readers, school library media specialists are not used to monitoring, tracking, and reporting student progress on an individual basis.

Large high schools with thousands of students present a special challenge to school library media specialists when it comes to acquiring individual knowledge of student learning. Students at the high school level tend to be enclosed behind subject teachers' classroom doors. Although accomplished school library media specialists at all school levels collaborate with classroom teachers to instruct students in information skills, and work one-on-one and in small groups with students to meet information needs, knowing the learning styles of each of several thousand students and developing instructional strategies to meet each of those student's needs sounds like a daunting task.

PROPOSITION FOUR
Teachers Think Systematically about Their Practice and Learn from Experience

A term now common in schools and colleges of education is *reflective practitioner*. Teachers are expected to continue to develop their professional skills long after their formal teacher training has ended. Reflection is a process of deep analytical thinking. It requires continual professional reading, thinking how best to implement changes that could improve student learning, and then applying the appropriate educational practices, along with continued analysis to determine the success of those practices.

Today's graduates of teacher education programs begin articulating their reflections on teaching practice from their very first course in their freshman or sophomore year of college. By graduation, and subsequent entry into the profession, they are skilled at analyzing and reflecting to improve their teaching. In contrast, experienced teachers, who may have long been out of graduate school, may find the art of reflective writing completely new. The concept of reflective practice is relatively new to the school library media profession and is just now beginning to be integrated into school library media preparation programs. School library media specialists may have to practice these skills to perform at the level expected of accomplished teachers.

PROPOSITION FIVE
Teachers Are Members of Learning Communities

Accomplished teachers are expected to function as members of professional communities at the local, regional, state, and national level. They are also expected to participate in professional education communities, as well as those in their subject field. The school faculty may represent one community, while the parents association may be another. Yet another will be a teacher's professional or subject-area association.

Library and information science professionals fully understand and engage in learning communities. The field has long had mature professional networks that share resources, data, and services among users. The concept of networking to share resources, merge data systems, and jointly share ownership of electronic databases is decades old. Professional association activity has always been seen as a professional responsibility from the point of entry into the profession. Library professional associations, now centuries old, have provided national standards, access to other professionals through professional conferences, and implementation strategies for best practices since their inception.

School library media specialists may be more comfortable in the professional networks of library science than in those of education, but both are required for the accomplished school library media specialist.

These five core propositions are the hallmark of the National Board Certified Teacher. The propositions are also finding their way into mainstream teacher education. The National Council for the Accreditation of Teacher Education (NCATE) provides the standards and accreditation procedures for most teacher education programs in the United States. NCATE recommends that master's programs in teacher education be aligned with NBPTS standards, thus fulfilling part of the third section in the NBPTS objectives, which is to integrate these high and rigorous standards into the American educational system for the preparation of teachers.

Achieving Certification

The process for becoming a National Board Certified Teacher is comparable for all teaching specialties. Standards have been written for fourteen teaching areas, and more standards are being developed for other areas.[10] Once the standards have been developed, a portfolio process is devised. Candidates for National Board certification prepare a portfolio in four areas. The first three areas are directly related to subject expertise, while the fourth area, Documented Accomplishments, is standard across certificates.

It is a reasonable practice for school library media specialists to work with NBPTS candidates in other subject areas in the preparation of their portfolio entries. The Social Studies area, at the Adolescence through Young Adult level, has as its first three portfolios Teaching Reasoning through Writing; Fostering Civic Competence; and Promoting Social Understanding.[11] The social studies teacher who stands in front of the classroom with tired overheads is not an accomplished social studies teacher, and may also prove resistant to collaborative information skills instruction. The accomplished social studies teacher working on his or her NBPTS portfolio, on the other hand, is most likely the type of teacher who can be a useful partner to the school library media specialist during the NBPTS candidacy.

Classroom teachers investigating the NBPTS process for their teaching area will have the same feeling of trepidation that school library media specialists feel. The bar for designation as an accomplished teacher is very high. Incorporating technology into instruction, providing inquiry and research strategies, or incorporating literature into the classroom are requirements for some subject area portfolio processes. The school library media specialist is a natural partner for these activities. The school library media portfolio process aligns nicely as well with that of the classroom teacher.

In addition to instructional strategies, nearly all of the subject portfolios require a videotape of classroom instruction. In many schools, operating the camera was the first introduction to NBPTS for school library media specialists. Helping classroom teachers achieve the "accomplished teacher" designation creates a natural payback process that can be resolved through the classroom teacher assisting the school library media specialist.

The portfolio entries may be on different topics for teachers in different subject areas, but the core principles on which the entries are based will be the same. All candidates share the same basic understanding of accomplished teaching, which must be evident in their portfolio entries.

After the portfolio is submitted, candidates sit for assessment center exercises. Candidates are given six questions integrating theory and practice in their area of expertise. Thirty minutes are given to answer each question.

Although the portfolio entries and assessment center exercises vary in scoring weight, candidates must achieve a 2.75 average score on a 4-point scale to achieve board certification. For the library media candidate, the first three portfolio entries are each weighted at 16 percent. The fourth entry, Documented Accomplishments, is weighted at 12 percent, and each of the six assessment center exercises is weighted at 6.67 percent. See figure 1-1 for the weighting of scores.

Candidates failing to achieve a 2.75 average score can "bank," or retain, individual parts of their portfolio and can retry just those entries on which they scored poorly. For instance, in figure 1-1, a candidate who scored a 1.75 on entry one in the portfolio section may wish to retake that entry, while banking higher scores in the other entries. Very rarely will a candidate want to retake the entire ten-part assessment. In most cases, a candidate will score highly in one area and not so well in others. Choosing which of the entries to retake is sometimes difficult. The score received on the retake entry eliminates the previous score. It is possible to score lower the second time, especially if a candidate does

FIGURE 1-1 ■ LIBRARY MEDIA SCORING WEIGHTS

PORTFOLIO	WEIGHT (%)
Entry One: Instructional Collaboration	16
Entry Two: Fostering an Appreciation of Literature	16
Entry Three: Integration of Instructional Technology	16
Entry Four: Documented Accomplishments: Contributions to Student Learning	12
ASSESSMENT CENTER	
Organizational Management	6.67
Ethical and Legal Tenets	6.67
Technologies	6.67
Collection Development	6.67
Information Literacy	6.67
Knowledge of Literature	6.67
TOTAL	100.02

Data obtained from the NBPTS Scoring Guide for Library Media, http://www.nbpts.org.

not truly understand and accept the deficiencies found in his or her entry the first time.

It is not recommended that candidates try to guess at which entry they will perform highest and give sole attention to that entry. Many times candidates are surprised when the scores are received, and they may have scored poorly on a section in which they considered themselves to be expert. It may be that candidates do not prepare as much for entries in which they feel they have a strong knowledge base. It is important to remember, though, that the entries are scored based on the standards. Past practice is not always best practice, and school library media specialists need to revisit what the field considers to be best practice. A thorough reading of and reflection on *Information Power* is the best companion to the NBPTS standards.

Knowledge or experience does not automatically create accomplished teachers. Accomplished teachers know and perform according to the five core principles. They know their students and their subject matter, they are expert teachers, they think about their practice, and they engage in the professional communities of the profession.

WHO ARE THE NBCTS?

Research has shown that a strong motivator to apply for NBCT status is the financial incentives that are available for successful candidates. In North Carolina, NBCT candidates have the $2,300 entrance fee paid by the state, are guaranteed several days off from school to work on their portfolio, and are given a 12 percent pay increase for the life of the certificate (ten years). At one time, North Carolina had over one third of the NBCTs in the country. This type of incentive is easier to accomplish if a statewide pay scale exists for teachers, as it does in North Carolina. In unionized states, in which each local negotiates with individual districts for pay increases, adding funds for candidate support tends to be scattered. Of course, NBCTs and unionization provide an interesting paradox. A union stance that "a teacher is a teacher is a teacher" is not conducive to admitting that merit pay, which is the basic premise of NBPTS certification, is desirable.

Figure 1-2 indicates the top ten states by their total number of NBCTs. North Carolina, as just mentioned, has by far the greatest number of them. As other states recognize the value of identifying accomplished teachers, the lead that North Carolina has over other states will shrink somewhat.

The figure shows the influence of strong state support for the NBPTS process. Governor Jim Hunt of North Carolina served on the first National Board and was instrumental in ensuring that North Carolina would, as the board suggested, identify accomplished teachers and reward them for staying in the classroom.

While North Carolina has had a

FIGURE 1-2 ■ *Top Ten States by Total Number of NBCTs*

North Carolina	8,280
Florida	6,364
South Carolina	3,866
California	3,080
Ohio	2,374
Mississippi	2,110
Georgia	1,780
Oklahoma	1,238
Illinois	1,083
Alabama	781
TOTAL FOR ALL STATES	40,209

As of November 2004. Figure prepared by NBPTS, http://www.nbpts.org.

long history of providing incentives for teachers to attempt the NBPTS process, other states are also offering monetary rewards. These rewards are in two categories: rewards for achieving NBCT certification and financial support to candidates for the certification process. These rewards vary widely by state, and in some states, by districts. South Carolina, for instance, increases the salary of NBCTs by $7,500 for the life of the certificate, while individual districts may increase that amount by a further $1,000 to $5,000. South Carolina will also pay 50 percent of the certification fee for candidates who submit scorable entries, and will pay the other 50 percent upon their achievement of NBCT status.

Figure 1-3 is a sampling of some of the incentives by states.

The figure shows some of the types of rewards or incentives, along with any financial support for the NBPTS process. Funds in either of the categories are dependent on state legislation, and are always subject to available funding. In addition, in those states in which individual districts set salary schedules, the types of financial arrangements are dependent on union contracts or district policies.

Although receiving both the designation of accomplished teacher and a financial reward is appealing to many teachers, the rigor of the certification process is an appeal to some school library media specialists but a deterrent to others. The sheer number of NBCTs in states such as North Carolina, Florida, or South Carolina is an emotional incentive. Support groups, mentor networks, and preparatory workshops are an important part of NBPTS candidacy. These are readily available in states with large numbers of NBCTs. Candidates in other states may have to travel to find help, or join online mentor networks.

FIGURE 1-3 ■ *Typical Incentives for NBCTs by State*

STATE	REWARD/INCENTIVE	FINANCIAL SUPPORT
Alabama	$5,000 annual salary increase	Certification fee paid for 75 candidates
Delaware	12% salary increase	Noncompetitive loan program, along with some state and district grants
Idaho	One-time bonus of $10,000, paid at $2,000 a year for 5 years. Some districts also have bonuses.	Provides up to $1,150 toward the fee. Some districts also have some funding.
Montana	One-time stipend of $3,000. Some districts will also award as much as $2,000 annually.	State will support 20 candidates at 50% of the fee
Oklahoma	Annual supplement of $5,000	Fee paid for 200 candidates
Washington	Annual salary enhancement of $3,500	Fee paid for 300 teachers

CRITICISMS OF THE NBPTS PROCESS

There has been criticism of the NBPTS certification as a white, suburban, female designation. The African American passing rate is of concern to many. Laura Onafowora, a recent doctoral graduate at the University of North Carolina at Greensboro, is among those who wonder if the African American teaching style is addressed by the NBPTS bias training.[12] In her dissertation, Onafowora identifies African American teaching styles as based in cultural traditions that exist for the purpose of transmitting values as well as academic content.

Onafowora compared the portfolio entries of six NBPTS candidates who were identified as exemplary teachers, although they did not receive passing scores on their NBPTS assessment. She found that the teaching styles used by these teachers could be perceived as more teacher-centered than the National Board assessors were looking for, as evidenced by the assessor comments on the portfolios of African American teachers who did not achieve board certification. Assessors made comments such as the teaching seems teacher-centered, does not allow for enough student input, or does not appear to be student-centered. There is little to no published information on the success rates of teachers in other minority groups in achieving National Board certification.

NBPTS strongly defends its assessor bias training. It notes that the training has never been found to be in question in clinical trials. NBPTS assessors are trained in identifying hidden biases and in learning to recognize identified biases as they assess. The problem of minority passing rates has not been solved at this writing.

The question of whether NBCTs are truly the best teachers is being debated as well. Cynics may wonder if the designation of "accomplished teacher" given by the National Board Certified Teacher label is really true. Does it make a difference for a child to be taught by an NBCT versus a non-NBCT? Proof of the efficacy of any one element in the educational process is always difficult to achieve, but there is some research that shows promise in this regard. The first major study, conducted by researchers at the University of North Carolina at Greensboro, found that NBCTs scored higher on elements of teaching than did other teachers. In addition, the study found that NBCTs tended to have higher student achievement levels than those teachers who attempted but did not achieve National Board certification. Other published research has found the same results.[13]

Current studies in progress will tell us more about this area. Lloyd Bond's oft-quoted study compared NBCTs with teachers who attempted National Board certification and did not achieve it.[14] He found that NBCTs did produce higher levels of student achievement. More research is necessary in order to accurately determine the impact that National Board certification has on the learning of students in America's classrooms.

SUMMARY

As previously noted, the three parts of the NBPTS mission are to identify high and rigorous standards for what teachers should know and be able to do, to identify a process whereby teachers can identify themselves as accomplished teachers, and to effect policy changes in teacher preparation and teacher supervision. To some extent, NBPTS has been successful in its mission.

The first three of the NBPTS's core propositions might be expected of any good teacher. We should certainly hope that good teachers care about students, that they have a thorough and in-depth knowledge of their subject, and that they know both how to teach and how to apply their teaching skills to their subject area. The last two propositions are what give a special meaning to the designation of National Board Certified Teacher. The accomplished teacher is expected to understand the process of student-centered learning, rather than just delivering instruction to a class of students. The portfolio entries require the teacher to demonstrate effective teaching by describing details of individual students' learning styles, and then showing how the instruction is modified as those students progress.

Accomplished teachers think about how they are teaching and how students are learning. They are constantly searching for ways to improve student learning by changing their teaching. Accomplished teachers actively seek professional growth opportunities for themselves and share their learning with others. They are active members of professional associations.

School library media specialists can be identified as accomplished teachers. In succeeding chapters in this part, we will look specifically at the school library media standards for National Board certification.

NOTES

1. National Commission on Excellence in Education, *A Nation at Risk: The Imperative for Educational Reform* (Washington, DC: Government Printing Office, 1983), 5.
2. In 1986 the first edition of *Information Power* (Chicago: American Library Association) was prepared by the American Association of School Librarians and the Association for Educational Communications and Technology. The second edition was published in 1998.
3. *Libraries and the Learning Society: Papers in Response to "A Nation at Risk"* (Chicago: American Library Association, 1984).
4. "School Library Media Programs and Their Role in Schooling: An AASL Response to the *Nation at Risk* Report," in *Libraries and the Learning Society*, 1–2.
5. Carnegie Task Force on Teaching as a Profession, *A Nation Prepared: Teachers for the 21st Century* (Carnegie Forum on Education and the Economy, 1986).
6. Abraham Flexner, *Medical Education in the United States and Canada: A Report to the Carnegie Foundation for the Advancement of Teaching*, Bulletin no. 4 (New York, 1910).
7. Carnegie Task Force, *A Nation Prepared*, 55.
8. Mission statement of NBPTS, http://www.nbpts.org.
9. The NBPTS website has a breakdown of NBCTs by year at http://www.nbpts.org/nbct/nbctdir_byyear.cfm. In addition, the NBCT directory can be searched by certificate and by year.
10. The NBPTS website has overviews of each certificate, plus the full text of the standards, portfolio instructions, and other helpful information.
11. Adolescence and Young Adulthood/Social Studies-History portfolio instructions, National Board for Professional Teaching Standards, http://www.nbpts.org/candidates/guide/04port/04_aya_ssh.html.
12. Laura L. Onafowora, "Measurement Consequences Reconsidered: African American Performance and Communication Styles in the Assessment for National Teacher Certification" (PhD dissertation, University of North Carolina at Greensboro, 1998).
13. Several studies have now been published regarding National Board Certified Teachers and student academic achievement. The most recent study is Leslie G. Vandervoort, Audrey Amrein-Beardsley, and David C. Berliner, "National Board Certified Teachers and Their Students' Achievement," *Education Policy Analysis Archive* 12, no. 46 (September 8, 2004), http://epaa.asu.edu/epaa/v12n46/v12n46.pdf.
14. Lloyd Bond et al., "Defrocking the National Board," *Education Matters* 1, no. 2 (Summer 2001): 79–82.

2 NBPTS and School Library Media

In the mid-1990s I met a friend, Sara Kelly Johns of upstate New York, at a professional conference. As we talked of our professional activities and caught up on the different aspects of our lives, Sara raved about a new committee she was on. It had regular meetings in Washington, D.C., and she swore it would change the profession. It was something about standards for teaching. She told me about their meetings and discussions about school library media specialists and the central importance of the act of teaching in our profession. She was adamant that these standards would give school librarians the equal peer status with classroom teachers that the field has always sought, and always fallen short of attaining.

"That's nice, Sara," I said, and never gave two thoughts about another committee that would probably produce a report that some people would read and that most would shelve or file. It was not until the first pilot cohort of library media specialists was testing the portfolio entries that I realized the significance of the NBPTS Library Media Standards Writing Committee.[1] Sara was right. That committee, these standards, and the NBPTS process could change everything.

BEHIND THE STANDARDS

The five core propositions described in chapter 1 are the basis for the accomplished teaching espoused by the National Board. Subject-specific standards are written by standards writing committees, which apply the NBPTS core propositions for effective teaching to the specific subject area. The Library Media Standards Writing Committee was one such subject-specific committee.

More than half of the members of any standards writing committee must be building-level practitioners in that subject area. The other half is usually a mix of university professors, district-level supervisors, and other specialists. In the Library Media Standards Writing Committee there were 3 university professors, 1 school principal, 2 library media supervisors, and 9 building-level library media specialists, one of whom was an NBCT under a generalist category.[2] The committee was formed in 1998, and the first cohort of library media specialists was ready to begin the NBPTS certification process in fall 2001.

More than Subjects

Each set of NBPTS standards has two equally important designations. The first reference is to the age level covered by the standards, and the second refers to the subject area.

NBPTS groups student ages in four categories:

- Early Childhood (EC), ages 3–8
- Middle Childhood (MC), ages 7–12
- Early Adolescence (EA), ages 11–15
- Adolescence and Young Adulthood (AYA), ages 14–18+

Figure 2-1 lists the available NBPTS certification areas. Note that for some subject areas, teachers have to choose a specific age range on which to focus. For instance, teachers of mathematics will choose either EA, meaning the middle school ages of 11–15, or AYA, for high school students of ages 14–18 or older. The standards are different because the students in those age ranges are different, and the way that mathematics is best taught varies by age level.

This sometimes narrow definition of an NBCT has an impact on school library media recruitment. States that provide incentives for teachers to stay in the classroom pay the reward or incentive as long as the NBCT is teaching in the NBPTS certification area. An NBCT generalist who moves to school library media will generally keep her incentive pay as long as she has remained with the same age group of Early Childhood or Middle Childhood. An NBCT who moves from a subject area into school library media usually does not keep that

FIGURE 2-1 ■ *NBPTS Certification Areas*

EC/Generalist	EAYA/English as a New Language
EA/Mathematics	ECYA/School Counseling
MC/Generalist	EA/English Language Arts
AYA/Mathematics	EA/Science
EMC/Art	AYA/English Language Arts
EMC/Music	AYA/Science
EAYA/Art	ECYA/Exceptional Needs Specialist
EAYA/Music	EA/Social Studies-History
EAYA/Career and Technical Education	ECYA/Library Media
EMC/Physical Education	AYA/Social Studies-History
EMC/English as a New Language	EMC/Literacy: Reading-Language Arts
EAYA/Physical Education	

Figure developed from NBPTS certification areas as of fall 2004, http://www.nbpts.org.

extra money. The reward/incentive is for the NBCT designation of a subject area. In some cases, the desire to become a school library media specialist has been strong enough for NBCTs to willingly lose their incentive pay. In other cases, however, classroom teachers receiving NBCT incentives have reluctantly withdrawn their desire to enter the school library media profession.

In NBPTS terms, the NBPTS library media standards are referred to as ECYA/Library Media. The library media standards are listed as Early Childhood through Young Adulthood, therefore ECYA/Library Media means that these standards reflect accomplished teaching for ages 3–18 or older in the area of library media. This is an important distinction. The NBPTS core proposition one states: "Teachers are committed to students and their learning." Accomplished teachers in library media should be able to show that they are competent in teaching to this wide grade-level area, and that they have a knowledge of learning styles, student needs and interests, and student motivations for children as young as age 3 and students who are over the age of 18. This is a challenge for any professional in any field, but it is a basic requirement for accomplished teachers in school library media.

This designation of such a wide age range is not unusual in the school library media field. For the most part, it matches school library media licensure requirements, which in most states is K–12. However, there are few library media specialists who are actively engaged in practice to the entire age range of

3–18 in everyday professional practice. Over time, school library media specialists naturally concentrate their personal professional growth efforts on the age group of the school in which they are working. This presents a special challenge to school library media specialists who are attempting NBPTS certification. High school library media specialists must relearn areas of service that affect early childhood. Elementary school library media specialists will have to look again at the range of literature, skills, and interests of high schoolers.

Teaching as a School Library Media Profession

Attention must also be drawn to the obvious. The NBPTS standards are prepared under the auspices of the National Board for Professional Teaching Standards. The importance of teaching in these standards cannot be overstated. The successful candidate seeking NBPTS certification in library media is a National Board Certified *Teacher* in the same way that successful candidates are designated in elementary education, English, social studies, music, and any other teaching area. The designation is not National Board Certified School Library Media Specialist. The ranks of school library media NBCTs encompass good teachers in the field of school library media.

The key word in the title *NBCT* is that of *teacher*. The standards, the portfolio entries, and the assessment center exercises are all focused on the teaching act within the library media center context. Candidates considering the NBPTS certification process should have a copy of *Information Power* in one hand and the "NBPTS Library Media Standards" in the other. Candidates must read the core propositions, library media standards, and portfolio entries and consider whether their professional work places them in the ranks of accomplished teachers.

The designation of accomplished teacher does not sit well with all school library media specialists. Some candidates may feel that important parts of their professional work life in the library media center are not considered in the certification process. Administrative tasks such as cataloging and processing, collection development, network administration, or webmaster duties that are not directly connected with classes of students using the library could easily fall into that category.

A few candidates in the first cohort of NBCT library media specialists even talked freely on the Yahoogroups discussion list about taking time from what some considered to be their real job, that of being a nonteacher.[3] As more candidates achieve the NBCT designation, that talk is rarely heard anymore. The negative stereotype of the stern school librarian feeding the alligators in the moat so that the media center's precious resources can remain forever protected is not only not a good teacher; that person is also not a good school library media specialist. Jean Brown and Bruce Sheppard use the analogy of a mirror image to compare the jobs of teacher and teacher-librarian. Their statement that "teacher-librarians, first and foremost, are teachers" should be the assumption that candidates hold going into the NBPTS process.[4]

This quote represents the argument of those who believe that all facets of the job of the school librarian are related to student learning, and that the NBPTS process merely targets the areas that are most directly related to that learning. Certainly the teaching of information skills and the encouragement of reading are conducted through direct student contact, and therefore should have a direct impact on student learning. The *Information Power* principles that deal with knowledge of resources, collection development, organization of the materials and the facility, and other program administration tasks that are conducted primarily in the workroom may not have such an obvious connection to teaching, but they may still have an indirect impact on student learning. The question of whether or not the NBCT designation is that of an accomplished teacher of library media or of an accomplished library media specialist was discussed in a recent *Knowledge Quest* article.[5] No resolution was found.

Library media was the first nonclassroom teaching specialty chosen by NBPTS as an area for certification. This brings high distinction, but also close scrutiny to the library media field. The debate has always raged as to whether school library media specialists should have experience as classroom teachers before they enter the school library media profession. Margie Thomas and Patsy Perritt's latest survey of school library media certification requirements notes that more states are changing their requirements to mandate classroom teacher licensure before entry into the school library media profession.[6]

Some feel strongly that school librarians with previous classroom experience have a better foothold for collaboration with classroom teachers, since they have "been there." It is felt that school library media specialists who were classroom teachers have a better background in curriculum development, assessment, and other areas.

Others feel that requiring subject teacher licensure before school library media licensure removes excellent candidates from the school library media profession. A forty-year-old might be willing to earn a master's degree in library science, but may not be willing to go through teacher licensure in a field in which he or she does not care to teach, simply to obtain the prerequisite licensure to then enter a preparation program for school library media. The field may be raising barriers for well-educated professionals desiring a career change who could become dedicated and excellent school library media specialists.

This also speaks to the debate over the preparation for school library media specialists. As late as 1984, Jane Ann Hannigan raised the suggestion that school library media training might be better housed in colleges of education than in schools of library and information science. She pointed out that it made more sense to train school library media specialists as teachers than to lump this specialty in with the more general education for librarianship. She also noted that library schools had no foundation in which to prepare teachers, and few faculty who had K–12 teaching experience.[7] Of course, the opposite side was taken by Peggy Sullivan in the same volume. Sullivan's view was that school library media education needed to remain part of the broad definition of library science education.[8]

State-level requirements for licensure also add fuel to the debate. Each state has different requirements for licensure as a school library media specialist. Some require master's degrees, others require postbaccalaureate training, and still others allow undergraduate degrees in school library media. The educational level of school library media specialists has never been a barrier to engaging in professional activities at the national level, however. The American Association of School Librarians has had presidents and board members representing all of the educational levels possible. All were considered equal partners at the table.

NBPTS certification will provide a research basis for comparison of these different requirements against the objective standard of the certification process. It will allow researchers to compare the education and training of school library media specialists with previous teaching experience, those from an MLIS versus an education school, and those who enter the field with a noneducation background. Debates of background, skills, experience, and training can now have objective instead of emotional rationales to support opinion.

Regardless of their educational background, number of years teaching, or professional on-the-job experience, school library media candidates entering the NBPTS process need to be aware that they will be judged by their teaching skills as applied to the best practices of the school library media field. They need to be aware of the latest educational theories and trends and be able to apply those practices to the school library media teaching classroom. Back issues of *Educational Leadership* and *Phi Delta Kappan* may have to be added to the stacks of *School Library Journal* and *Booklist* for evening and summer catch-up reading.[9]

Focus on Students

There is a tendency in the library world to focus on the stuff that makes up a library. Books and other print resources, audiovisual resources, and electronic resources make up our library collections. Facilities must be designed to allow the maximum use of these resources. Policies and procedures must be organized to fulfill the responsibilities of the library and information science professions to ensure open access to information, respect for privacy, and other ethical and legal considerations.

All of these are structural considerations. The topic of interest is the building blocks, real or virtual, that are the basis of good library service. When discussing good libraries, the inevitable question is: "What do they have?" The question may widen to incorporate policies and practices, and focus on how the resources of the library are circulated, accessed, and used, but the question and subsequent answer are still structurally based. The patrons are rarely front and center in the discussion.

This is not to say that the library world disregards the user. Quite the opposite is true. There has always been a focus on the user as the recipient of the stuff in libraries. The mission of *Information Power*, "to ensure that students and staff are effective users of ideas and information," sets the stage from the beginning for the focus of school library media programs. Training in the use of the reference interview and the selection process stresses matching the resources in libraries to the needs of the users. The NBPTS standards turn this process around, however. While the library world perceives the person as the end user, NBPTS sees the resources, facilities, and policies as the end use. It is a complete turnaround in focus.

First and foremost in the National Board certification process is the student. In the case of library media standards, the student may be anywhere in age from 3 to 18 years or more. The child is a product of and functions in a learning environment, partly as a result of home and community life, and partly by the design of the teacher. There is a need to teach that child, usually in conjunction with a group of other children. There is also a curriculum designed with that child in mind.

The degree to which we know and understand that child is the basis of a teacher's knowledge and skill and is the most important or even the sole criterion for success in teaching. Certainly in the National Board process, knowledge of the student is the most important criterion and is the foundation of all of the other skills.

The Library Media Specialist as a Teacher of Children

In order to be a successful candidate for NBPTS certification, the school library media specialist must be a skilled teacher and have the ability to focus those skills on students from ages 3 to 18 or older. With the wide range of ages that this represents, the school library media specialist must stay attuned to educational processes affecting all age and grade levels. This may mean a large chunk of time spent catching up on professional reading and an understanding of educational practices before beginning the NBPTS process.

It should be noted that there were school library media National Board Certified Teachers before the ECYA/Library Media Standards were written. School library media specialists could choose to be certified under one of the generalist areas in the age range. It is not known how many school library media specialists elected to be nationally board certified in this area.

Figure 2-2 shows the top ten states in the number of school library media NBCTs as of November 2004. Note that North Carolina has by far the greatest number. As discussed in chapter 1, this is usually attributed to the financial rewards that are in place in North Carolina to reward and support National Board certification. However, it also cannot be denied that mentoring and support networks have been an important part of the library media profession. North Carolina school library media specialists have been watching their teaching peers in the classroom obtain NBCT designations for years. They were eager to join those ranks and prove themselves.

FIGURE 2-2 ■ *Top Ten States by Total Number of School Library Media NBCTs*

North Carolina	278
Florida	200
South Carolina	131
Georgia	79
Mississippi	58
Oklahoma	37
Virginia	28
Illinois	25
Alabama	21
Louisiana	21
Washington	21

Figure prepared by the author from data available on the NBPTS directory of NBCTs, http://www.nbpts.org.

In other states with fewer NBCTs in classrooms, school library media specialists have had to learn about NBPTS and its mission in isolation from such a strong statewide support network. Figure 2-3 shows the number of school library media NBCTs in the remaining states.

FIGURE 2-3 ■ *Numbers of School Library Media NBCTs in Non–Top Ten States*

Kentucky, Ohio, California	16–20
Arkansas, Kansas, Hawaii, Maryland, New York, Arizona, Delaware, Missouri, Wisconsin	11–15
Minnesota, New Mexico, Pennsylvania, Rhode Island, Alaska, Connecticut, Iowa, Montana, Nevada, West Virginia, New Jersey, Colorado, Maine, Nebraska, Oregon, Texas, Utah, Vermont, Wyoming	1–5
Idaho, Michigan, North Dakota, South Dakota	0

Figure prepared by the author from data available on the NBPTS directory of NBCTs, http://www.nbpts.org.

Obviously, the population of the states has little to do with the number of school library media NBCTs in them. Besides financial factors in terms of state- or district-level rewards and support, another factor that helps determine the number of NBCTs could be simple word of mouth. In the top ten states, there are enough library media NBCTs to have a presence at conferences at the district level and in state organizations. Upon receiving the NBCT designation, school library media specialists may be honored at school and district events or noted in the professional association newsletter. New NBCTs excited about the process may host conference presentations at which they give tips and support to prospective candidates. A school library media specialist in one of the top ten states has a fairly good chance of knowing someone who has gone through the certification process, or one who can be a partner to go through it together. A school library media specialist in one of the four states in which there are no NBCTs will have to go through it alone. This makes a difference.

In fall 2002 the American Association of School Librarians attempted to mitigate that difference by hosting a forum on NBPTS certification. Each state affiliate was asked to send a team of one school library media representative from higher education, one affiliate leader, and one building-level library media specialist to the forum. As a direct result of that forum, the AASL hosts an interest group of NBCTs and candidates, and an NBPTS committee to hold events and inform the AASL. This group meets regularly at conferences and is open to all interested school library media specialists.[10]

What the figures cited earlier do not show are the numbers of candidates who have attempted but not achieved NBCT status. We do not know which of the portfolio entries or assessment center exercises are toughest for school library media specialists, or whether there is a difference in success/failure rates depending on grade level served, educational background, or years of experience. Ongoing research will clarify some of the questions.

In the meantime, the list of school library media NBCTs continues to grow. Over 750 school library media specialists attempted certification during the first year it was available. A total of 435 succeeded, which is an astounding pass rate. Each year the numbers grow, both in the number of school library media NBCTs and in the number of states with at least one successful candidate.

SUMMARY

When the Library Media Standards Writing Committee was formed, the wheels were set in motion for a change process that is still unfolding. The standards focus on the teaching act embedded within all areas of school library media best practice. The library media standards, portfolio entries, and assessment center exercises focus on the teaching act with students between the ages of 3 and 18 or older. This wide age range is parallel to the broad K–12 teaching certification awarded to school library media specialists in most states.

The emphasis on the student in the design, delivery, and assessment of instruction is the hallmark of NBPTS, and of good educational practice. School library media specialists in very large schools, or even in very small ones, may be daunted at the responsibility of designing instruction that meets the needs of each child. How one child learns, which is the heart of evidence-based practice at schools, is the heart of National Board practice as well.

It's not the thousand students in the school who matter; it's the one in front of you that counts.

Food for Thought

Are you a teacher? Start making checklists of the educational practices you incorporate in your teaching. Are you a constructivist? Do you espouse or eschew Direct Instruction? What is the educational philosophy of your school and district? What are the types of instructional methodologies commonly used in professional growth workshops? The purpose of your checklists will be to establish a professional reading list. From the "Food for Thought" box in chapter 1 you have started your professional reading. Now you can begin to research and target your reading.

How many school library media NBCTs are in your state? Search the NBCT directory to find out who they are and where they are. Begin a contact list.

Did your state AASL affiliate send a team to the AASL Fall Forum? If so, have you attended any follow-up workshops conducted at the state or regional level? Contact the affiliate to ask what help they can offer you and other school library media candidates.

NOTES

1. The members of the NBPTS Library Media Standards Writing Committee were Sharon Coatney, chair; David Loertscher, vice-chair; Jacquelyn E. Crook, Paula Galland, Ann Gilreath, Robert J. Grover, Sara Kelly Johns, Cindy Jolley, Bob Kaplan, Erlene Bishop Killeen, Lena Murrill, Mary Lou O'Conner, Karen Whetzel, Cynthia Wilson, and Nancy Zimmerman. For a complete list of their affiliations, see p. 49 of "NBPTS Library Media Standards" on the NBPTS website, http://www.nbpts.org.
2. Although the first class of library media NBCTs obtained certification in 2001, it had previously been possible for school library media specialists to obtain certification under one of the generalist categories. For instance, elementary or middle-school

library media specialists could obtain certification as early or middle childhood generalists. It is unknown how many school library media specialists had achieved certification and been designated accomplished teachers before the school library media certification was available.

3. The Yahoogroups librarymedia discussion list (http://groups.yahoo.com/group/librarymedia/) is considered one of the premier mentoring and support networks for candidates. The list was developed by Cynthia Wilson, NBCT, who was on the Library Media Standards Writing Committee.
4. Jean Brown and Bruce Sheppard, "Teacher-Librarians: Mirror Images and the Spark," chap. 9 in *Foundations for Effective School Library Media Programs*, ed. Ken Haycock (Englewood, CO: Libraries Unlimited, 1999), 79–88.
5. Gail K. Dickinson, "National Board Effects on School Library Media Education," *Knowledge Quest* 32, no. 3 (January/February 2004): 18–21.
6. *School Library Journal* regularly publishes updates on school library media certification nationwide. For the latest discussion, see Margie J. Thomas and Patsy H. Perritt, "A Higher Standard," *School Library Journal*, December 1, 2003.
7. Jane Ann Hannigan, "Vision to Purpose to Power: A Quest for Excellence in the Education of Library and Information Science Professionals," in *Libraries and the Learning Society: Papers in Response to "A Nation at Risk"* (Chicago: American Library Association, 1984), 51.
8. Peggy Sullivan, "Libraries and the Learning Society: Relationships and Linkages among Libraries," in *Libraries and the Learning Society*, 136.
9. *Educational Leadership* (Association for Supervision and Curriculum Development) and *Phi Delta Kappan* (Phi Delta Kappa) are two of the more popularly read practitioner journals for education. *School Library Journal* and *Booklist* are considered more library-related journals for school library media specialists.
10. See http://www.ala.org/ala/aasl/aboutaasl.

3   The ECYA/ Library Media Standards

Print out a copy of the standards, and follow along in the text as you read this chapter. You might highlight sections of the standards in different colors. Use one color for areas in which you are confident of your knowledge and skills, and another for areas that you may need to investigate further.

The NBPTS library media standards follow the same format as the standards for other subject areas. The ten standards are divided into three areas, following the headings of what library media specialists know, what they can do, and how they grow as professionals. There will always be some overlap to the standards when following this format, since what teachers do naturally comes from what they know, and how teachers grow as professionals stems from what they know and can do.

The most common flaw in reading the standards is to read for the main idea, skipping over all of the phrases that could be interpreted as less important. This is how students are taught to read. This training starts in the early elementary grades and is emphasized in reading comprehension tests at all grade levels. Even as adults, when note-taking or abstracting, it is a common practice to note only the main ideas. The NBPTS standards cannot be read in this way. Every word and every phrase has meaning.

For example, the first sentence in the introduction to Standard One: Knowledge of Learners is the following: "Accomplished library media specialists use their knowledge of human growth and development, their understanding of children, adolescents, and adult learners; and their familiarity with learning theories to work effectively with students of all ages, abilities, and learning styles in a variety of settings."[1] It may be tempting to glean from this sentence that accomplished teachers need to be familiar with all ages of learners and learning theories, note that carefully, and move on. This omits crucial points from the statement, however. Accomplished library media specialists, in that one sentence, are expected to do the following:

- Have knowledge and understanding of the following:
    human growth and development
    child learners
    adolescent learners
    adult learners
    learning theories
- Use that knowledge and apply it to the following groups:
    students of all ages
    students of all abilities
    students exhibiting all learning styles
- Demonstrate that the work they do with each of these groups is effective and that it is applied in a variety of settings.

Note-taking skills are usually a way to shorten one's reading of a text to an organized outline of main ideas. When reading the NBPTS standards, however, note-taking should tend to elongate the text, so that every point is covered. Figure 3-1 has some tips to use when reading the standards.

Information Power provides a visual picture of the NBPTS standards in action. Candidates beginning the certification process may want to make a copy of the *Information Power* principles listed after each of the *Information Power* roles.[2] As you read each standard, highlight the *Information Power* principles in a specific color. Then read the *Information Power* chapter that corresponds to each principle. The reflection goal is to merge your thinking about the NBPTS standards and *Information Power* principles with your reading of best practices in the library and education fields. What is a school library media specialist supposed to know, do, and be like? What does it look like when that is happening?

WHAT LIBRARY MEDIA SPECIALISTS KNOW

The content knowledge that library media specialists possess comes from three areas: knowledge of students, knowledge of the field of education, and knowledge of library or information science. Formal undergraduate and graduate edu-

FIGURE 3-1 ■ *Tips for Reading the NBPTS Standards*

1. Have freshly printed copies of the NBPTS standards on hand. After a period of time, pages will be covered in margin notes, highlights, and underlines. Keep the used version, but switch to a clean copy every so often. This will keep your perspective fresh, and the clean copy can be used as a comparison to the used version to see if your perception has changed.

2. Write down your reflections after each reading session. As your work with the NBPTS process continues, you will want to capture your thoughts, especially those at the beginning of the process. Keep a notebook handy to jot down phrases that can be used as reflection prompts.

3. Mark the standards freely. Use different colored highlighters to make statements stand out, scribble in the margins, and draw arrows and underlines. Make the process physical.

4. Read often. Replace the summer beach reading with a copy of the standards. Every time you reread, you will see something you missed before. Remember that scoring rubrics are based on the standards. It's easy to gloss over important points the first few times.

cation add to this combined knowledge base for most of the other certificate areas, but the extent to which that is true for school library media varies. Standards one to three are the following.

Standard One: Knowledge of Learners

Standard Two: Knowledge of Teaching and Learning

Standard Three: Knowledge of Library and Information Studies

School library media specialists are usually trained in one of three ways. They may have an ALA-accredited MLIS degree with school library media courses; they could have a master's of education program recognized by NCATE through AASL; or they could have an undergraduate teaching degree in the field of school library media, which is still possible in some states. There are, of course, variations on these, and the situation is muddied still further by the alternative licensure routes through the No Child Left Behind legislation.[3]

To prepare for the rigorous certification process based on the NBPTS standards, library media specialists will need to review the texts used in graduate study in each of the three knowledge bases listed above. Although journal reading is important, current journal articles discussing trends may not have the in-depth background information necessary for full understanding. Library media specialists will need to self-assess their knowledge, and then seek out ways to refresh their learning. Figure 3-2 suggests some college coursework in

FIGURE 3-2 ■ *Review of Knowledge Bases*

KNOWLEDGE BASE	TYPICAL COLLEGE CLASSES
Knowledge of students	Educational psychology Human development Diverse learners
Knowledge of education	Educational foundations History or sociology of education
Knowledge of library science	School library administration Collection development Library services and curriculum

which these knowledge bases are usually covered. Texts in these courses are not difficult to find; they are available in any college bookstore, even long after the semester has started. Stop by a nearby campus and browse to find the current texts. It may be possible to pick up some used texts very cheaply.

Standard One: Knowledge of Learners

Piaget, Bloom, Vygotsky. These names, along with those of other learning theorists, are crucial to the understanding of how children learn and develop. Piaget is well known for his studies of the development of thinking in children. Bloom's taxonomy guides most educational preparation. Vygotsky, less well known until recently, developed the "zone of proximal development" concept that is the basis for constructivism.

A thorough knowledge of students as outlined in standard one is crucial to a successful candidacy. In the portfolio process, candidates will have to discuss individual students and their learning. This can cause some degree of consternation for candidates, especially those in large schools. How can one person know the learning styles, home environment, and exceptionalities of 2,000 students in a large high school? Although it is conceivable that a classroom teacher over the course of the year can get to know a class of students to the depth that the standard requires, it is less obvious that a library media specialist, even in a relatively small school of 500 students, can do the same.

Learning styles are specifically mentioned in the standards and in the portfolio entries. This is an area in which library media specialists need to have a thorough knowledge and understanding, and it is one not usually covered in depth in school library media preparation classes. As with each of the standards, the need to know enough to fulfill all parts of standard one can be overwhelming. Library media specialists need to read this standard carefully and identify the essential pieces of knowledge. It may help to use the following as a self-test.

Do I understand the concept of learning styles in students?

Do I know and can I discuss basic child development in terms of learning theory?

Can I apply what I know about learning styles and child development to specific students?

Having an in-depth knowledge of each student in the entire school is not necessary. What is important is that the library media specialist understands the concepts of learning styles and learning theories and can apply them to students when teaching. Learning happens one child at a time. It doesn't matter if there are 2,000 students in the school or only 200. It's what a teacher knows about the child in front of him or her that matters.

School library media specialists are uniquely qualified to meet this standard because they can view students through a different lens than classroom teachers can. The library media center can be a safe haven for students who have problems fitting the mold of the good student. Because of this, school library media specialists can develop a rapport with students, and they sometimes know, more than anyone else in the school, about a student's life outside school, and about the student's life inside school but outside the subject learning process. School library media specialists develop this rapport with students over a number of years; this is far different from the classroom teacher who sees only a snapshot of the student at a specific grade level and sometimes only in a specific content area.

Standard Two: Knowledge of Teaching and Learning

Whether teaching is an art, a skill, a craft, or a science is still hotly debated in education circles. Some people may be born with an innate personality and aptitude that make it easier to become a good teacher, but accomplished teachers still must have more than the personality attributes of a sense of humor, patience, and a love of children. Teachers must understand and apply the principles of pedagogy.

Accomplished teachers know the building blocks of the act of teaching, which consist of a knowledge of learning theories and principles; the design and delivery of instruction, including the assessment of student progress in learning; classroom management; and basic curriculum development. The general knowledge in this standard applies to the profession of teaching and the field of education painted with a broad brush. Teachers are expected to understand the principles of curriculum development and the theories and practices behind the relationship of curriculum to classroom practice.

For school library media specialists, some of whom may have had little training in educational principles and practices, a knowledge of teaching is literally a foreign language. Just understanding the jargon may be a challenge. Understanding the full significance of educational trends such as increased high-stakes testing, zero tolerance effects on dropout rates, and other issues may require in-depth study.

NCATE refers to topics such as these as pedagogical "knowledge and skills."[4] Knowledge of these educational theories and practices is important, but that's not enough. "Professional pedagogical knowledge and skills" denotes the theories and practices as applied to specific subject areas. Curriculum development, for example, is an important pedagogical skill. The knowledge of curriculum development as applied to integrating the information skills curriculum into subject curricula is an important library media professional pedagogical skill. It is this merger of theory and practice that accomplished teachers have as reflective practitioners. The integration is best achieved in collaboration with the school community; the collaboration is itself a hallmark of school library media best practice.

Classroom management practices that are tried and true for the classroom teacher are different when applied in the library media center. Students in the classroom are scheduled into a fairly strict routine and are contained in a single room for a set period of time. This allows behavior management techniques to be applied on a regular basis and over a long period of time. Classroom teachers can work with individual students on behavioral issues and can develop a behavior management routine that can cover the entire day, week, or longer. The school library media specialist does not have that luxury. Students in the library media center may come in once each week or month, but for entirely different purposes, lengths of time, and under differing teacher supervision. Even the experienced classroom teacher who moves to a new career as a school library media specialist must learn new behavior management techniques.

The delivery of instruction is also very different in the library media center than in the classroom. In the library media program, students may be taught in large groups, small groups, or individually. Instruction may be delivered directly and face-to-face, with a library media specialist in a traditional teaching role. Instruction may also be delivered indirectly through learning centers, pathfinders, or other forms of self-paced instructional guides. All of these instructional activities could be happening simultaneously in a busy library media center. The school library media specialist is literally the facilitator of learning.

School library media specialists are uniquely qualified to meet this standard. Student-centered instructional strategies are a survival technique in a busy library media center. Teacher-directed activities in the school library media center would quickly result in only one class or one group using the library at a time, thereby denying access to the rest of the school. The accomplished school library media specialist learns how to multitask learning opportunities for students. This requires a knowledge of the best instructional strategies, a knowledge of the curriculum, and the possession of a repertoire of classroom management strategies that can operate as the glue that makes these differing processes effective.

Standard Three: Knowledge of Library and Information Studies

The library media program itself must be organized around best practices of the field, including cataloging and technical services, management strategies such as planning and budgeting, and evaluating library services and programs. Along with this core knowledge, the standard also addresses three major parts of the job role of the school library media specialist: literature, technology, and information skills. This standard has frequent "see also" references to other standards, which reflects the generalist nature of the library science field. This is a broad standard, covering the knowledge required to do the job of a school library media specialist. It is natural that this standard will overlap with other standards that cover what accomplished school library media specialists do and how they grow as professionals.

It is expected that school librarians have a thorough knowledge of children's and young adult literature. They should understand the criteria for quality literature and can apply those criteria to select literature based on the needs and interests of students. School librarians know the categories and criteria for award-winning literature and strive to maintain a balanced collection that includes award-winning resources when appropriate. School librarians also understand that the definition of the term *literature* applies to more than just books. It includes films, recordings, and videos, as well as magazines and some electronic resources.

Information skills processing is dealt with in a more comprehensive fashion in chapter 5 of this book. For now, it suffices to say that school library media specialists should understand information skills processing in students of all ages. Common research methodologies such as Big6 and I-search and researchers such as Carol Kuhlthau and Barbara Stripling should be familiar names.[5]

School library media specialists should also have an understanding of the technological foundations of the modern school library. The job description of the school library media specialist is not synonymous with that of a technologist, although many school library media specialists possess the skills to function at a very high level with technology. All school library media specialists need a basic understanding of hardware, software, and connectivity. They should understand the basic pieces of computer hardware, have an understanding of the software available, and know how to put these all together to make them work as an information-processing tool.

Summary of Standards One to Three

Although the NBPTS library media certification is based on the skills of effective teaching, the context for those skills is the library and information science field. School library media specialists have a foot in both professions. They carry the precepts, principles, and practices of teaching into the library field; and they carry the principles, precepts, and practices of library and information science into the education field. It is not a situation that calls for wearing two hats. It is fashioning a new hat out of the fabrics, styles, and couture of both fields.

In standards one to three, NBPTS outlines the knowledge that accomplished school library media specialists should have in the three areas of students, education, and library or information science. In the next group of standards, this knowledge will be applied to the practice of school librarianship: what accomplished school library media specialists do.

WHAT LIBRARY MEDIA SPECIALISTS DO

Simply possessing knowledge is never enough. The successful library media NBCT must also be able to demonstrate application of the best principles of education and library or information studies. Standards four to six, which are listed below, outline the skills required for designation as a library media NBCT.

Standard Four: Integrating Instruction
Standard Five: Leading Innovation through the Library Media Program
Standard Six: Administering the Library Media Program

Standard Four: Integrating Instruction

Chapter 5 will review the best practices of collaborative information skills instruction; however, a brief review of the precepts in this standard is needed here. Since the earliest research on information skills and inquiry learning, it has been understood that students best learn skills that they can apply at the time of learning. Hannah Logasa's 1928 example of collaborating with English teachers by taking the name of a literary character and researching that character's period, occupation, and fashion would still be appropriate today.[6] Worksheets, Dewey decimal skills sheets, and tests on how to use the index of an encyclopedia are useless in teaching students how to use information skills. Information skills must be integrated into instruction. There are three parts to this integration: co-planning, co-teaching, and co-assessment.

CO-PLANNING

Co-planning means merging the library media curriculum with subject curricula. It means serving on curriculum committees and establishing a media advisory committee to advocate for collaborative information skills instruction and the integration of the library program into all facets of the school. Co-planning happens at the curriculum development stage as well as at the point of instruction. It happens at the idea stage, the implementation stage, and the evaluation stage.

CO-TEACHING

Co-teaching does not necessarily mean teaching in unison, or even teaching in the same room, whether the instruction is taking place in the library media center or the classroom. Co-teaching means teaching toward the same merged teaching goal, having an understanding of what students can learn, and realizing the shared importance of the information skills integrated into classroom instruction.

Resource provision has an important role in the delivery of instruction. The library media specialist must be aware of resources for all learning styles, abilities, and in all formats. Specific examples used in this standard are large-print books, technology resources, and resources for different ability levels.

CO-ASSESSMENT

Co-assessment in its simplest form is simply the culmination of a unit so integrated that at its completion, it is impossible to decide which assessment pieces belong to the classroom teacher and which to the library media specialist. After planning and teaching an integrated unit together, sharing the assessment of student learning progress of that unit only makes sense.

School library media specialists are not usually expert in assessment. Whether because of the sheer number of students that they see on a daily basis, because many of the information skills are informally taught, or because some skills such as encouragement of reading are hard to assess, school library media specialists cannot generally give specific information about the learning of individual students. This is an area that will need some background work before taking the National Board assessment. One aid may be the widely used book *Understanding by Design*, a favorite for planning assessment strategies.[7]

School library media specialists are uniquely qualified to meet this standard. The integration of resources and information skills instruction into the content curriculum has been, since the beginning of school libraries, one of the most important functions of the school library media specialist.

Standard Five: Leading Innovation through the Library Media Program

To say that libraries have integrated technology is an understatement. First audiovisual equipment and resources and then computer technology have changed the way that libraries do business. Almost every library routine is affected by technology in some way. The management and organization of libraries is computer-based. Resource provision relies on computer technology, and information skills encompass a range of computer and other technology skills as well. Although books are still prevalent and encouraging children to read remains one of the most powerful reasons why school library media specialists enter the field, there is no doubt that innovative uses of technology also prove to be a career draw.

Technology must be defined as more than just computer hardware and software. School library media specialists should be experienced in the areas of assistive and adaptive technology, and be aware of the instructional uses of technology not commonly used in school, such as the iPod or gaming simulations. Technology has always entered the school through the school library. If a school had only one computer connected to the Internet, one piece of audiovisual equipment, or even just one telephone outside the main office, chances are that these would be placed in the school library.

But while school library media specialists are usually technophiles, they are not strict technologists, attracted to the gimmickry and gadgetry of electronic toys. Standard five uses the phrase *visionary leadership*. School library media specialists use technology as a tool. They use technology to create more access to more resources by more members of the library community.

School library media specialists teach the efficient use of technology. They do this not just, for example, by teaching PowerPoint as a skill, but by teaching how PowerPoint can be used to enhance and extend the learning process. Technology has the ability to cover a range of learning styles. School library media specialists are skilled at matching those learning styles to the most effective and efficient technology.

School library media specialists are uniquely qualified to meet this standard. When technology entered school libraries in the mid-1960s, the school library became the leader in using audiovisual materials. Later, when computer technology appeared on the horizon, the school library media profession effectively integrated computer technology into program administration, information access and delivery, and the integrated instruction of information skills.

In many schools the school library media specialist is charged with maintaining all technologies, along with teaching the use of those technologies. More and more schools are hiring technicians to keep the equipment running and technology facilitators to teach the use of the technology. This allows the school library media specialist to concentrate on integrating the use of the technologies in the instructional program.

Standard Six: Administering the Library Media Program

Everyone knows one. There is one in every district: a library media specialist who sees her job as feeding the alligators in the moat surrounding the school library in an effort to protect the library's resources. Simply by holding the key to resources, and by holding those resources hostage, the school library media specialist has a degree of power over the rest of the school. There are two ways to use that power. One is to say no, and to create policies and procedures to deny access and to organize the library so that the resources remain intact, similar to ancient insects encased in amber.

Of course, the other way to use power is to say *yes*, to use the power to create policies and procedures that open access to the library. This type of school library media specialist engages the library media advisory committee in planning the library media program, and develops the program around a stated vision and goals. Accomplished library media specialists also engage the library media advisory committee in evaluating the progress of goal implementation and program development. They also manage the media program so that the greatest number of resources can be used by the greatest number of people.

School library media specialists are uniquely qualified to meet this standard. From the first days in library school, the ethical attributes of the profession such as open access to information, user-centeredness, and an understanding of the library's place in the local community are reinforced in a variety of ways. School library media specialists are trained to plan, develop, implement, manage, and evaluate the library media program within a developed community of supporters.

Summary of Standards Four to Six

This set of standards represents the heart of best practices in school library media centers. More than any other passionate cry from the field, standard four sets out our role as a teacher of information skills. The terms *teacher-librarian* or *library teacher* are becoming the state licensure terms in some states, notably California. Calling ourselves teachers has always been stressed, but it is even more effective when the National Board for Professional Teaching Standards refers to school library media specialists in this way.

This set of standards also states clearly and unequivocally what school library media specialists do. They teach. They innovate the education process through the integration of print, nonprint, and electronic technologies and forms of access. They manage the library program so that it is essential to the learning of students.

The first set of standards (standards one to three) identified the unique aspects of the school library media specialist in the role of teaching children. The second set (standards four to six) places those unique roles within the context of the instructional and organizational life of the school. The next set, the last four standards, brings the school library media specialist into the school and library communities.

HOW LIBRARY MEDIA SPECIALISTS GROW AS PROFESSIONALS

This group of standards reflects the school library media profession as a community within larger communities. Library media specialists are a community of professionals. Professional associations such as the American Library Association and the American Association of School Librarians function as member-driven communities with strong national conferences, active discussion lists, and functional committee work.

In this set of standards, the school library media specialist is responsible for setting an agenda of personal professional growth. The fact that there are four standards in this area emphasizes the importance of lifelong learning for the school library media NBCT. Standards seven to ten are the following:

Standard Seven: Reflective Practice

Standard Eight: Professional Growth

Standard Nine: Ethics, Equity, and Diversity

Standard Ten: Leadership, Advocacy, and Community Partnerships

Standard Seven: Reflective Practice

This standard has two elements. The first calls for self-reflection: a constant searching for ways to improve personal skills, create increasingly innovative strategies for teaching, and become adept at an ever-widening river of technology. Library media specialists agonize about how to become better at what they do. They see innovation demonstrated at conferences, and they think about ways they can improve their own professional skills. They read professional journals and keep up with literature in the field. And finally, they ask questions and seek answers from other school library media specialists as they engage in study to increase their knowledge and skills.

This reflection is not just about personal skills. School library media specialists also think deeply about their programs. They learn from others and from experience, and they make conscious decisions about the directions for their programs. In a constantly changing educational environment, the school library media specialist must be aware and engaged in personal change to meet the challenges of that changing environment, and to assist school staff as they meet the challenges as well.

School library media specialists are uniquely qualified to meet this standard. With most states requiring a master's degree for entry-level certification, school library media specialists enter the field with strong academic qualifications, perhaps more than any other school staff member except for the principal. The conferences, journals, and professional meetings in the field are planned for learning as well as information-sharing. Librarianship truly is a lifelong learning profession.

Standard Eight: Professional Growth

It was once said that school library media specialists are the "teachers of teachers." Although this statement is tinged with arrogance and obfuscates the role of the school library media specialist as a teaching peer, it is nevertheless true that personal professional growth for the school library media specialist extends to a responsibility to offer professional growth activities for others in the school community as well. Very few others in the school have this high level of responsibility for schoolwide professional growth as strongly as does the school librarian, perhaps only the building administrator.

It is expected that school library media specialists plan and implement strategies for their own professional growth. They take courses and workshops, attend conferences, read professional journals, and actively engage in the communities of practice for school library media specialists. Some of these communities are electronic ones, such as the active discussion lists of LM_NET and

AASLFORUM.[8] Others are face-to-face, such as committee work and district or regional meetings.

School library media specialists also work for the professional growth needs of others in the school community. They attempt to discern those needs by observation and analysis, by conversation and listening to others. They plan activities, purchase resources, and work to effect school change that will benefit the school community along with the library media program.

School library media specialists are uniquely qualified to meet this standard. The decision to enter the school library field is for many of them a midlife decision. Because of that, school library media specialists tend to be determined learners and active participants in the profession. The responsibility to advocate for the school library program is congruent with the need to offer assistance to students, parents, other teachers, and administrators for their professional growth needs.

Standard Nine: Ethics, Equity, and Diversity

This standard speaks to the basic premise of library and information science. It would be difficult to find a recent or not-so-recent graduate of any library school who could not recite chapter and verse on intellectual freedom, rights to privacy, basic copyright information, and other legal and ethical issues. Librarians in the general sense are concerned about access, ethics, and diversity, all of which are interrelated.

Although this topic is discussed further in chapter 8, in general, it can be said that there are four types of access: emotional, physical, economic, and intellectual.

Emotional. Do students want to come into the library media center? Do they find resources there that they want to read, are interested in using, and that reflect who they are? Do those resources also reflect the world that students face outside the school walls? Do they believe that their interaction with the library and its resources is valuable?

Physical. Can the students find the library? When parents walk in the main entrance to the school, is there signage that indicates that a library exists, and gives directions to it? When new students enter the school, does signage point them to the library as they walk in the hall? Is the signage only in the language used in the school, or will parents and students see the library sign in all languages represented in the student body? Are issues of patrons with special needs addressed, including books and resources shelved too high or too low, doors too hard to open, or desks that do not accommodate wheelchairs?

Economic. The only way to never have to pay a fine for overdue materials is never to check anything out. That should not be the first rule that parents tell their children about libraries. Paying for copies, for library use, for forgetting a pencil, all of these are barriers for children of poorer families. To a lesser extent, book fairs sometimes may highlight the economic barriers to information, even when books are reserved for donation to children who cannot afford to buy one. School library media specialists using book fairs to bring new books to children who may never have set foot in a bookstore need to ensure that giving children new books is done subtly and confidentially. Otherwise, not only is it made obvious that some children can buy books and others cannot, but this humiliating fact is reinforced by charity.

Intellectual. Does the collection match the reading level of the users? Are the books too hard, too easy, too long, in the wrong languages, and so on? Part of intellectual access is instructional. Students must be taught to use materials, encouraged to read by removing limits on the numbers of books they can check out, and be given open access to all formats.

School library media specialists are uniquely qualified to meet this standard. Although other types of librarians can blithely accept as instructed the tenets of ethics, equity, and diversity, school library media specialists have the extra responsibility to serve in loco parentis, literally "in the place of parents." In no other type of library do the staff have to wrestle with tough ethical issues such as filtering versus child safety or what teachers and parents want their children to read or not to read, to the same degree as school librarians do. Rushworth Kidder, in his book *How Good People Make Tough Choices*, points out that ethical dilemmas are not right versus wrong. Instead, they are usually right versus right.[9] School library media specialists wrestle with the ethical dilemmas of providing open and equitable access to highly diverse school populations every day.

Standard Ten: Leadership, Advocacy, and Community Partnerships

School library media specialists must advocate for their programs in order for them to thrive, but also even for them to simply survive. It would be wonderful if an understanding of the goals and vision of the school library media program were so ingrained in the consciousness of the school community that advocacy and leadership roles were not necessary. Unfortunately, this is not the case. While we may bemoan the fact that school principals do not receive training in what a school library is supposed to be, cooler heads would ask: why should they? School administrators do not receive training in guidance, biology, industrial arts, technology, or any other part of the school curriculum either. They receive training in legal issues, such as testing, special education guidelines and requirements, and other broad concerns of education today. The role of the school library media specialist is to place the library's program at the heart of the principal's goals.

Several recent publications such as the AASL's *Principal's Manual* can be used to help the school library media specialist strengthen the school library program.[10] Although this brochure is intended for the building principal, school library media specialists can use it as a self-assessment tool to teach a building administrator how to see the success of the school library program in action.

Standard ten also reflects the responsibility of the school library media specialist to form formal networks and informal linkages with other libraries and with community resources such as museums, organizations, and individuals. The importance of family, both immediate and extended, and the family's role in encouraging library use as a lifelong habit, also fall under this standard.

School library media specialists are uniquely qualified to meet this standard. The concept of the library as an "electronic doorway" works both ways, both as an access point for the school community and as an entry point for select resources outside the school.[11] The doorway is electronic in several ways. First, the atmosphere is electric and alive with the buzzing of information access. More literally, the information may be found in electronic format through automated libraries, electronic databases, and other ways of accessing information.

SUMMARY

The NBPTS core propositions are the basis for all subject standards. The standards then draw from those core propositions to articulate specific behaviors desired in National Board Certified Teachers. For the library media professional, these standards draw from both education and from library and information science.

The NBPTS standards are divided into three areas: what library media specialists know, what they do, and how they grow as professionals. The standards cover the knowledge bases of child development, education, and library science. They outline the basic job role of the school library media specialist in integrating instruction, in the encouragement of reading, and in the use of technology as an information tool. The standards recognize that the unique position of the school library media specialist in the school requires a high level of reflection and evaluation that results in constant professional growth, both personal and schoolwide. The basic premises of ethics, equity, and diversity ensure that school library media specialists become leaders in the school community, advocating for students through library media services and forming partnerships with other institutions and individuals to assist in this effort.

Food for Thought

Practice identifying learning styles. Before a class enters, pick a number out of a hat, and match that to your plan book to identify a child. While teaching, observe the learning of that child. Reflect in your journal on how that child learns. Match your reading of learning styles with what you see. Do this with no more than one class every few days, so that you have time to think and write in depth about that one child.

Reading the NBPTS standards can be overwhelming. Sometimes it helps to remember what we're good at doing. At the end of each standard in this chapter, there is a paragraph that starts, "The school library media specialist is uniquely qualified to meet this standard." Why are you uniquely qualified to meet this standard? Write a reflection about why you are good at what you do. Use examples and stories about specific students. You will be surprised at what you know.

Now that you have read the core principles and the standards, reflect on how they reinforce each other. Make posters for your NBPTS personal space so that the standards and the core principles are always in front of you.

FURTHER READING

Dewey, John. (Various works.) Note: Many of John Dewey's works are in the public domain, and others have been reprinted.

John Dewey wrote prolifically in the late nineteenth and early twentieth centuries on a wide range of topics, but candidates will be especially interested in his writings on inquiry learning. Some of Dewey's most valuable writings are *How We Think* (New York: Heath, 1933), *Democracy and Education* (New York: Macmillan, 1916), and *The School and Society* (Chicago: University of Chicago Press, 1900).

Haycock, Ken, ed. *Foundations for Effective School Media Programs.* Englewood, CO: Libraries Unlimited, 1999.

Haycock's edited work provides an overview of collaborative teaching and learning, including planning and integration, the delivery of instruction, and the structural supports needed for a collaborative integrated library media program.

Kuhlthau, Carol Collier. *Seeking Meaning: A Process Approach to Library and Information Skills.* 2nd ed. Westport, CT: Libraries Unlimited, 2004.

Candidates seeking to understand the Information Search Process will find this book invaluable. Kuhlthau reviews the theory and research behind her process, and then applies the process in scenarios based on her research. Candidates should place this book at the top of their reading list.

Loertscher, David V. *Taxonomies of the School Library Media Program*, 2nd ed. (San Jose, CA: Hi Willow, 2000).

Stripling, Barbara, and Sandra Hughes-Hassell, eds. *Curriculum Connections through the Library*. Westport, CT: Libraries Unlimited, 2003.

> Both this book and Stripling's earlier work (*Learning and Libraries in an Information Age*, 1999) focus on inquiry learning as a component of the integrated library program. This will be a companion read to the Kuhlthau book above.

NOTES

1. National Board for Professional Teaching Standards, "NBPTS Library Media Standards,"http://www.nbpts.org, p. 7.
2. The principles specific to each of the *Information Power* roles are found in *Information Power: Building Partnerships for Learning* (Chicago: American Library Association, 1998), 58, 83, 100.
3. No Child Left Behind legislation allows teachers in some states to be considered highly qualified in areas other than those in which they have received formal training by passing a state licensure test. Some universities have sought to mitigate the impact of this by offering alternative, much shorter routes to licensing.
4. For more information on the NCATE standards, see the NCATE Unit Standards athttp://www.ncate.org. NCATE also has standards developed by the AASL for the preparation of school library media specialists.
5. Although each information skills processing and research methodology might need to be reviewed separately, a good place to find a quick overview is in Ken Haycock, ed., *Foundations for Effective School Media Programs* (Englewood, CO: Libraries Unlimited, 1999).
6. Hannah Logasa, *The High School Library: Its Function in Education* (New York: Appleton, 1928). See also Elsa Berner, *Integrating Instruction with Classroom Teaching at Plainview Junior High School* (Chicago: American Library Association, 1958), for a later example of collaboration.
7. Grant P. Wiggins and Jay McTighe, *Understanding by Design* (Alexandria, VA: Association for Supervision and Curriculum Development, 1998).
8. LM_NET is a huge school library discussion list hosted at listserv.syr.edu. Currently the list has over 17,000 subscribers. AASLFORUM is the electronic members-only forum for the American Association of School Librarians.
9. Rushworth M. Kidder, *How Good People Make Tough Choices: Resolving the Dilemmas of Ethical Living* (New York: Morrow, 1995).
10. The *Principal's Manual for Your School Library Media Program* brochure is available from the American Association of School Librarians.
11. In the late 1980s and early 1990s, New York State's Division of Library Development designated libraries with a high level of technology integrated into the curriculum through the school library media program as Electronic Doorway Libraries. For more information, seehttp://www.nysl.nysed.gov/libdev/edl.

4

The NBPTS Certification Process

From the beginning, the goal of NBPTS was to create a rigorous process to identify accomplished teachers, and by all accounts it has succeeded. Recent research on the effectiveness of National Board Certified Teachers indicates that students achieve at higher levels with NBCTs than with those teachers who attempted the process but did not achieve NBCT status.[1] However, the rigor of the certification process cannot be ignored. Achieving accomplished teacher status on the first try is not at all guaranteed, and nearly half of all candidates retake some part of the process for a second or third try. Some candidates cannot achieve National Board Certified Teacher status even after three tries.

The word *failure* is sometimes used to denote the lack of achievement of NBCT status, but that is a misnomer. Most candidates who attempt National Board certification swear that it is the best professional growth process they have ever been through and, achieved or not, was worth the effort. There is some support for the contention that there are more NBCTs in states and districts that financially reward teachers for achieving NBCT status.[2] However, candidates have been known to say that although one may start out spurred by the promise of financial reward, the rigor of the process must be driven by an internal desire to achieve.

BANKING

Candidates who do not achieve NBCT status on their initial attempt can bank high scores and retake individual sections to achieve the required 2.75 overall score. Because of this, and because of the rigor of the process, becoming an NBCT is considered a three-year process, but for the purposes of this book, we will consider it a four-year process, as shown in figure 4-1.

FIGURE 4-1 ■ *The Four-Year NBPTS Process*

Year One	Review, study, and organize
Year Two	Attempt the process
Year Three	Bank high scores, and try again
Year Four	Bank high scores, and try again

Year one is spent learning about the process, conducting self-analysis to learn more about areas of particular need, and perhaps contacting other candidates to get an understanding from them. Year two is the first year of application, completing the ten-part assessment. If all goes well, the process stops there. However, if the average score did not reach the required 2.75 for passing, the process can continue. The candidate can bank (retain) his or her highest scores in particular elements, and retake those sections in which the lowest scores were received.

The following year, some candidates most likely have passed. However, candidates who were unsuccessful may still choose to bank another set of scores and try again the following year. Now that attempting NBPTS certification is available on a rolling basis, it is possible to think of semesters instead of years. A candidate can spend one semester preparing, one semester in process, and then spend succeeding semesters (or longer) retaking those sections in which he or she received low scores.

In the first cohort of National Board library media candidates, "bankers," those candidates who did not receive passing scores, rarely announced their presence on the Yahoogroups librarymedia discussion list after the first set of scores had been released. Some did express their anger, frustration, shame, and other emotions, but most were silent. However, after the second year, several of these previously silent but now successful candidates came forth and discussed their experiences. This created more discussion and openness, as current bankers began to make their plans for retaking certain sections. The successful NBCTs who could not only empathize but could also share their own personal experience of first failure, and then success, reassured candidates who had not done well in a particular entry.

Attempting National Board certification means a risk of failure, something that we try to avoid in everyday life. Although taking risks by trying to learn to ski or to swim or do something else new is not uncommon, NBPTS certification is based on the basic building blocks of our profession. This is stuff that we are already expected to know how to do. However, NBPTS discussion lists and candidate support training stress that being a skilled teacher is not enough. NBCT candidates prepare portfolios and engage in assessment center exercises for the purpose of articulating clear, convincing, and consistent evidence that they can perform at the accomplished teacher level. Failure to provide that evidence can stymie even the most accomplished teacher, regardless of skill. The evidence that a candidate provides is all that the assessor can use to determine if the candidate qualifies for NBCT status.

In the school library media field, most professionals work alone. Contact with other school library media specialists is rare, and therefore, so is comparison of skills. An English department of twenty-five teachers may have in its midst experienced mentors, newbie teachers just out of school, and fast-track hotshots. An English teacher thinking about attempting National Board certification can compare his or her personal strengths and weaknesses as a teacher with colleagues, and can see that all teachers may have some stellar qualities, as well as failings. School library media specialists, who may see others in the district once a month at most, are not usually able to engage face-to-face with other school library media specialists. It is thus more difficult, even for the most professionally active school library media specialists, to compare their job performance at the holistic level with their peers in other schools.

For school library media specialists, attempting NBPTS certification requires a special capability for risk-taking. School library media specialists may not be aware of their professional competence going into the NBPTS process, and they may feel more isolated while in the midst of the process. Most of us are also better risk-takers in private than we are in public. We may try downhill skiing and laugh at our mishaps, but self-esteem is rarely involved.

In contrast, the NBPTS process is very public. Peers, students, parents, and administrators will know that a candidate is attempting National Board certification. So will a candidate's family. The effects of the NBPTS process inspire jokes on the discussion list about endless pizza dinners, lack of family time, and understanding and supportive children and spouses. Everyone knows that a candidate is attempting board certification. They know, especially, because candidates must obtain signed parental permission forms to videotape teaching.

Students, parents, and colleagues will know when the scores are released, and they will ask questions. "Did you pass?" is a question that will be put to candidates at every turn after scores are announced.

Students, even at the older levels, usually have a high perception of a teacher's ability. The concept that a teacher can fail at an intellectual exercise, especially one in the teacher's subject area, has probably not occurred to them. Banking candidates may find it difficult to reconcile their personal situation with the concept that NBPTS failure is an excellent chance for teachers to show students that it is okay to fail, but it is not okay not to try. Under the same circumstances, students would be pushed forward, even if we knew that their chances of success were slim. However, when those same circumstances are applied to adults, it can be seen that teachers may have more difficulty dealing with feelings of failure.

The NBPTS process thus offers teachers an opportunity to model the importance of risk-taking in the learning process. Students can see how the processes of test-taking, assignments, studying, and portfolio development are done by adults. It makes the learning process transparent. The logistics of the NBPTS process also create an opportunity to demonstrate the importance of margins, labels, titles, and proper credit for work. Students can see that there are real-world applications for parameters that they may have to show in their own schoolwork. Otherwise, they may consider the logistics of assignments as just another teacher whim.

THE PROCESS

There are two parts to the NBPTS certification process: first are the portfolio entries, and then the assessment center exercises. After registering, the NBPTS candidate will prepare four portfolio entries. The first three are specific to the subject area, but the fourth, Documented Accomplishments, is universal to all subject entries. For that entry, teachers in all subject areas show how their accomplishments have improved their teaching, and therefore improved student learning.

The second part of the process is the assessment center. After completing and submitting the portfolio entries, candidates take six tests, each lasting thirty minutes. The questions relate to the content area of the candidate. Each exercise poses a question related to content, then reveals a scenario for the candidate to answer the question in context.

Preparation

Preparing for National Board certification is a four-year process. The first year, candidates should read widely in the literature of their field, focusing on teaching and learning processes. Simply unpacking the box and beginning the entries will be difficult without developing one's background knowledge. The following areas should guide the reading.

FOCUS ON STUDENT LEARNING

All NBPTS certificates are twofold in what they designate. The first descriptor reflects the developmental level of the student, as noted previously. For school library media specialists, the developmental levels are early childhood to young adulthood (ages 3–18+), referred to as ECYA. It is not accidental that developmental levels are the first descriptor. A knowledge of students from ages 3 to 18 is of primary importance for school library media NBCTs. This presents a learning challenge for the school library media field. Knowledge of student learning styles is not always covered thoroughly in school library media preparation programs. For school library media specialists who do not have an undergraduate education degree or a master's degree in education, very little of their formal preparation concentrates on how students grow, learn, and develop.

Even if learning styles and differentiated instructional methods are reviewed in preparation, adapting instruction to meet exceptionalities, children of diversity, and others in the teaching of information skills is not covered. The standards for teacher preparation used in the reviews conducted by the National Council for the Accreditation of Teacher Education separate pedagogical knowledge and skills (how to teach) from pedagogical content (how to teach a specific subject).

There is a pedagogical content knowledge for the teaching of information skills. There are also learning styles associated with that teaching. Without the focus on individual student learning and pedagogical content knowledge in preparation, school library media specialists must work hard to keep up with their teaching peers.

PEDAGOGY

School library media specialists wear many hats in the school. The 1998 edition of *Information Power* stressed the role of teacher, along with that of instructional partner. As emphasized earlier, standards are prepared by the National Board for Professional Teaching Standards. The focus of the preparation is on accomplished teaching. School library media specialists must be accomplished in all aspects of teaching, including lesson planning, instructional delivery, and assessment of student learning.

Collaboration with classroom teachers, for decades the accepted best practice of school library media information skills instruction, is an important context, but the school library media specialist's knowledge and skills in the act of teaching apart from that context must also be strong. Specific skills in the act of teaching include the design of instruction, the development of lesson plans, delivering instruction, adapting instruction to increase student learning, and then the assessment of instruction, both within the lesson to be able to adapt instruction and after the lesson to assess student learning. The ability to reflect on instruction for the purpose of continual improvement is also necessary.

What the National Board Requires

Along with knowledge of student learning and pedagogical skills, there are other skills areas represented by the NBPTS process. It has been said that an accomplished teacher can find the NBPTS process too much of a hurdle, that it takes too much time, and it forces a teacher to document processes that to experienced teachers are routine.

The NBPTS process has also been described as a professional growth experience in itself, rather than just a test of knowledge and skills. In fact, it is both. It is a test, but it is also a learning experience. It forces a teacher to articulate not just the *what* of teaching and learning, but also the *why* and the *how*. The National Board Certified Teacher must be able to articulate and model the attributes of the accomplished teacher. Sometimes, this involves isolating and articulating concepts long assimilated in the act of good teaching.

The four stages of competence, a concept widely circulated in business circles, are listed in figure 4-2.[3] The first stage, unconscious incompetence, could be described as blissful ignorance, when one is not aware of what one does not know. At the second stage, anxiety and discomfort are awakened, as one is now aware that there is something unknown. In stage three, the learner has mastered the concept. Stage three is sometimes described as a sixteen-year-old with a driver's license, overconfident that he or she knows everything there is to know about driving. The final level, stage four, occurs when the concept becomes so natural, so ingrained, that it is difficult to explain the skill to another.

Accomplished teachers operate at the last stage, unconscious competence. Accomplished teachers have traveled the stages of competence by the awkwardness of being inexperienced, the blustering overconfidence of several years, and

FIGURE 4-2 ■ *Four Levels of Competence*

Stage 1	Unconscious Incompetence	Stage 3	Conscious Competence
Stage 2	Conscious Incompetence	Stage 4	Unconscious Competence

finally the accomplished stage of unconscious competence. First-year teachers are placed with experienced teachers for several reasons, one being that it is easier to simply watch and learn from an accomplished teacher.

The NBPTS process forces a teacher to return to the beginning. Accomplished teachers attempting the NBPTS process quickly pass the blissful ignorance of stage one. They become aware of their own faults and failings and of omissions in their preparation programs, and they develop a plan of study to again achieve unconscious competence.

Some candidates are surprised that they may receive their lowest scores in an area that they consider to be a professional strength, and the example of the sixteen-year-old driver could be the reason why. It is fairly simple to be confident about what one knows, especially if one never learns the gaps, weak areas, and missed opportunities within that knowledge.

Being simply a good, above-average, or even an excellent teacher is not enough. In order to present clear, convincing, and consistent evidence, an accomplished teacher must have above-average organizational skills, be a stickler for detail, be comfortable with videotaping in front of and behind the camera, and be able to write reflectively.

ORGANIZATION

"I have to mail this tomorrow and I am short two bar codes!! How did this happen!"

Upon achieving candidacy status, each candidate is granted a number, which must appear on all of the individual pieces sent in with the portfolio. Candidates will be sent bar codes with their candidate number. The number of individual pieces, including videotapes, samples of student work, written reflections, and other documented sources of evidence, can number more than fifty. Nothing could be worse than the disaster mentioned above, when candidates are working close to the deadline and realize that they have lost an important component of the portfolio.

Along with keeping track of pieces such as bar codes, candidates also have to keep the entries themselves organized. Many candidates use milk crates and folders to keep track of stuff. Extreme stories of organization include candidates who have declared a room in the house (usually the dining room) off limits to everyone except themselves, so that they can keep the boxes of evidence and the various piles undisturbed.

Of course, another problem in the above scenario is the timing. The candidate exclaiming over the loss of bar codes noted that the portfolio had to be mailed the next day, and more than likely the electronic lament was sent close to midnight. The portfolio will be expected at its destination on a specific date.

There is usually much discussion on lists as to the latest possible pickup time with the major delivery companies so that the box can arrive before the deadline. One has to ask, if a candidate has spent hundreds of hours, missed family times, and spent sleepless nights preparing to send this box, why would he or she take any chances that the box would be late arriving?

As noted recently in the *Chronicle of Higher Education*, a similar tragedy unfolded when it was noted that the University of California–Berkeley campus would not have any Fulbright scholars in 2004. The problem was not the lack of qualified candidates, but rather a missed pickup. The package was ready and waiting at 4:00 p.m. on the stated day, but the delivery driver did not appear. The applications were late. The quality of candidates is irrelevant if the materials do not arrive on time.

The following tips may be helpful in keeping materials organized.

In the pre-candidacy phase, organize by standards. Use individual boxes or milk crates and file folders.

Label everything. Make sure that correct cites are listed on all copied articles. Carefully note the date, time, and place of anecdotes and other evidence.

When the box arrives, inventory the contents to make sure that you have everything that you need. If you are missing anything, contact NBPTS immediately.

Stay physically organized. Put the bar codes, instructions, and any other necessary forms somewhere where they can remain undisturbed. Periodically, especially when you need a break, re-inventory your materials. It will give comfort to know that you are ready in one small aspect of your candidacy experience.

Read carefully all directions in terms of margins, fonts, length, and so forth. Stay well within the limits given. You do not want your entry discarded or parts of it unread because you were trying to save a quarter of an inch by using an unfamiliar font.

Set personal deadlines well ahead of NBPTS dates. Plan to mail the portfolio entries at least the day before you absolutely need to send them. Losing them in the mail means a semester of hard work down the drain.

Review your organization periodically. Is everything labeled, organized, and filed? As you move through the process, you may want to change the organizational structure from standards to portfolio entries and then to assessment center exercises. Regardless, organization is key to the process.

Follow the directions. As simple as that sounds, it is reported as one of the major reasons why NBPTS status is not achieved. Double-check all margins, fonts, length of videotapes, and other style and logistical notes. Check to make sure that you have followed the writing prompts and answered the questions asked.

VIDEOTAPING

"Videotape early and videotape often" seems to be a good phrase for NBCT candidacy. In spite of the concern felt over the videotape, it is only a required part of two entries in the portfolio. The main concern when approaching the videotaping of one's teaching is to fulfill the requirements without wasting both candidate preparation time and student learning time in getting it perfect. It is expected that the videographer is not a professional, but more likely another candidate or a professional peer. Some school library media specialists have used spouses, other teachers, or even students to operate the video camera. In larger school districts, there may be a videographer employed by the district. The norm, however, is to use a willing "someone" who is close at hand. Candidates have had success using a student, the school secretary, the collaborating class-room teacher, or their media assistant. One story had a candidate using the school secretary, who was called at mid-lesson back to the office. The tape showed a brief consultation, a wobble as the camera was secured on the tripod, and the video went on. The best lesson may not have the perfect video, but as long as the video shows the clear, convincing, and consistent evidence of accom-plished teaching required by the entry, its use should be given serious consider-ation, despite any technical flaws.

There are even reasons not to hope for a perfect product. The perfect lesson, with perfectly behaved students and a well-coiffed teacher in control, may be so smooth that there are no writing "handles" attached. What better way to show accomplished teaching than at times when things do not go exactly as planned? In one of the entries, candidates must choose two students and show their learning progression. Watching the videotape may help choose which students to use. A lesson with teachable moments and interruptions may show the ability to teach far more than an isolated Stepfordesque class.

This is especially true for school library media specialists who work with little or no clerical assistance, under a fixed schedule, and with high demands made on them by classroom teachers. There are stories of frustration from having to stop the tape (and therefore making it unusable) to deal with interrup-tions. Sometimes school library media specialists are so used to catering to the immediate gratification of classroom teachers that they forget they have control over how they choose to spend their time.

A former student, when showing the author a collaborative teaching episode required to be videotaped for class, explained with great frustration why she felt she could not incorporate collaborative information skills instruction into the school library program. As we were watching the tape the phone rang off-camera, and in the middle of teaching the lesson, the school library media specialist disappeared into the office to answer. "There," she exclaimed, "that happens all the time." My question back to her was obvious: "Why did you answer it? Wasn't what you were doing with the students more important than anything the caller wanted you to do?"

This doesn't mean that the school library media specialist should not serve the teachers. It does mean that an inexpensive answering machine with the message, "I am teaching a class now. Please state your request and I will help you as soon as this class is finished," may gain more respect from classroom teachers than the self-martyred school library media specialist with a scarlet V for Victim on his or her chest.

Videotaping is a perfect opportunity to show the NBPTS assessors how accomplished school library media specialists translate interruptions to teaching into only minimal interruptions in student learning. In the middle of teaching, when a classroom teacher walks to the front of your class—on camera—and asks for a particular resource or to schedule a class, answer the question briefly, point to the camera, and note that you are taping your National Board entry and will get to it right after class, and then continue.

The preceding scenario is an excellent way to illustrate the context of the problem. Every classroom teacher has exceptional students, and this is generally acknowledged. However, every classroom teacher also has structural exceptionalities, with a schedule, room location, afternoon sun or heat, morning cold, and other areas in which accommodations for learning must be made. School libraries are no different. School library media specialists report instances in which their facilities are next to the lunchroom or have no walls, and there are always a few classroom teachers in the school who think nothing of interrupting class. These exceptions to the perfect instructional organization are an expected part of school life.

The important piece of the NPBTS process is to be able to demonstrate how you are an accomplished teacher in spite of all of the exceptionalities you may face. Having these instances appear on camera is an opportunity to use that example in your description. It's an illustration, and as such, is priceless.

Keep in mind that the important part of the videotape is the degree to which the assessor can find the clear, convincing, and consistent evidence to award a high score. It is completely unimportant how the candidates look in the video. That it was a bad hair day, that the dress chosen to wear added at least fifteen pounds, and that its color is obviously wrong for you will not affect your score.

Some candidates, in situations where the tape ran out, was not in the machine, or in some disastrous situation in which the tape becomes unusable, will retape the same class, with the same lesson. There have been anecdotes of classes that have been asked to stay after school, when silence in the halls could be counted on, so that a class could be repeated. Although the candidate was pleased with the result, it is difficult to imagine that there is much spontaneity here, either in the teaching act or in the learning process. Answers will become rehearsed, the teaching will become too smooth, and the artificiality of the atmosphere may come through. It is probably a better idea to videotape several different classes, and then decide by watching the videos which one will best allow you to make your chosen points. Think of the difference between reading a speech and speaking from notes. No matter what the reader does, it is obvious when a speaker is reading a speech.

There is some equipment in which a candidate may want to invest. Obvious needs are a video camera and a VCR on which to transfer the video to the standard ½-inch format. A tripod is handy to keep the camera steady, and a PZM microphone has been found to be best at picking up student conversation. Although the videotaping works best if the videographer can move about the room to focus on students as they work, if no one is available for this, then a tripod can be used.

Candidates may want to practice with different types of equipment and with different sound connections to plan which one works best. Microphones pick up and amplify sounds amazingly well, some of which we do not want to have on the tape. If the air conditioner suddenly roars to life and drowns out the talking of students or teacher, the tape is unusable. Figuring out where the camera should be and what microphone to use far outweighs the decision of who the videographer should be.

One school librarian reported using another teacher to videotape until he was called unexpectedly to the office. The librarian calmly walked to the camera, aimed it carefully, and walked back to continue teaching. That's how a good teacher handles interruptions of any sort, refusing to allow anything to get in the way of student learning.

WRITING

One criticism of the National Board certification process is that it is a writing test.[4] Although accomplished teaching certainly remains the fundamental criterion of the NBPTS process, there is no doubt that the clear, consistent, and convincing evidence required to achieve that status is provided through writing.

The "reflective writing" used in National Board preparation is divided into three parts: description, analysis, and reflection. One of the major reasons that teachers do not achieve NBCT status is because of their writing. Certainly one would think that the grammar, spelling, sentence structure, and language usage of teachers would be mostly correct, and that is probably true. The real problem is in the use of description, analysis, and reflection. The NBPTS portfolio entry instructions give a detailed explanation and illustration of reflective writing. The following are brief summaries of each type.

Description

Description paints the contextual picture of the scene. It gives details that happened before the instructional process or event and background information on the class, school, or organization. Description then moves to the present, and gives the details that the reader must know in order to see what unfolded in the instructional sequence. Description paints a logical order of events and places the reader in the scene.

Description answers the questions "what, when, and who?" After reading a description of an instructional event, the assessor should know the goal of the lesson, the strategies used to teach the lesson and assess student learning, and the context of the school and class. The assessor should be able to understand the setting in which the NBPTS candidate is able to give clear, convincing, and consistent evidence of accomplished teaching.

It is difficult to know with descriptive writing whether the writer is giving too much information or not enough. Will the reader be overwhelmed with minute detail, or will the reader be missing crucial information? The suggested page limits given in the portfolio entry instructions should give the writer some help in this regard. The most common error in descriptive writing is neither too much nor too little information, however. It is the failure to move past description to the next level: analysis.

Analysis

Analysis answers the questions "why?" and "how?" In instructional contexts, analysis tells the reader the degree to which the students learned, whether or not the instructional strategies used were successful, and how the lesson may be improved the next time. Analysis takes the description and pulls it apart to reset the facts in the context of future instruction.

Reflection

In the NBPTS instructions, analysis and reflection are paired. For our purposes, however, reflection might be best understood as a separate term. Reflection answers the question, "what next?" Reflection takes analysis and moves it to the next level. Analysis tells how much the children learned; reflection wonders why that is. Analysis redraws the instruction so that it could be more effective next time. Reflection gives an understanding of why the teacher thinks this might be true.

A simplistic definition of reflective writing is that description is "what," analysis is "so what," and reflection is "now what." This type of writing is difficult to begin under a deadline. Those people who are in the habit of writing journals tend to be better at reflective writing, since they are used to thinking about the larger picture.

Reflection takes practice. When a candidate begins to think about applying to NBPTS, he or she should also begin reflecting about the instructional process.

SUMMARY

It has been said that even the best teachers sometimes do not manage to become an NBCT, and that may well be true. The logistics of organization and the ability to not only write well but also to write reflectively can be major stumbling blocks. This relates back to the stages of competence. The unconsciously competent teacher must go back to the beginning and become conscious of every step of the teaching process.

Food for Thought

Write a letter to yourself before you begin the NBPTS process. Think about why you want to do this, what you hope to gain, and what you think about the work that it takes to become a school library media NBCT. Promise yourself that should you not achieve NBCT status on your initial try, you will nevertheless continue the process. Put the letter away and don't read it until the day after you send the box to NBPTS. Then keep reading the letter until you receive your scores.

Set a time for videotaping your teaching and then do it. Concentrate on the mundane, such as the tape being rewound in the machine and the sound working. Immediately after taping, make a copy. Steel yourself with comfort foods and watch the tape, promising to look at the class, not at yourself. Review the NBPTS prompts for each entry, and find the places in the video that illustrate exactly what you want to show.

Start writing every day. Study the NBPTS portfolio instructions for reflective writing, and critique your own writing. Did you describe? Did you analyze? Did you reflect? As practice, set a standard of one-third description, one-third analysis, and one-third reflection for every page.

NOTES

1. See Leslie G. Vandervoort, Audrey Amrein-Beardsley, and David C. Berliner, "National Board Certified Teachers and Their Students' Achievement," *Education Policy Analysis Archives* 12, no. 46 (September 8, 2004), http://epaa.asu.edu/v12n46/v12n46.pdf.
2. Joyce Lieberman, "The Future of Teacher Compensation: Linking Salary to National Board Compensation" (presentation, Mid-Western Educational Research Association, Columbus, OH, October 16–19, 2002).
3. The concept of the four stages of competence is copyrighted by at least three training service agencies. A search for the concept's origin proved fruitless, with some companies insisting that it was invented by a middle-level manager, others by a CEO, and a search of the literature found only circular references.
4. Robert Burroughs, "Composing Standards and Composing Teachers: The Problem of National Board Certification," *Journal of Teacher Education* 52, no. 3 (May-June 2001): 223–32.

PART II *Best Practices*

So far this book has examined the rationale, context, and background of the National Board for Professional Teaching Standards. In part 1 we started with a review of the inception of the National Board, and the rationale for creating this rigorous voluntary process for identifying accomplished teachers, and then moved on to the core principles of accomplished teaching, the library media standards, and the process of becoming a National Board Certified Teacher.

Later, in part 3, we will review the portfolio entries and assessment center exercises involved in the application process for library media NBCT status. Before we do that, however, it would be wise to review some of the basic premises of school librarianship. The NBPTS certification process can be viewed as a test of best practices in school librarianship as viewed through the lens of teaching. Part 2 reviews the background of each concept and principle that will be discussed in detail in the context of the portfolio process in part 3.

We will begin with the basic instructional premises of school librarianship. Chapter 5 reviews the collaborative teaching of information skills. Chapter 6 follows with the encouragement of reading, and chapter 7 covers the integration of technology. Chapter 8 then gives an overview of other best practices, including advocacy, flexible access, and other access principles.

This part covers the background research and application of the basic principles of school library media instruction. Each chapter includes an operational definition applied to today's school library media program, reviews current research, and suggests further reading on the topic. In each chapter as well, reflective writing prompts will be included to guide the candidate's thinking toward the portfolio entries and assessment center exercises.

Collaborative Integrated Instruction

5

Information skills are best taught in collaboration with a classroom teacher and when integrated into classroom content. This best practice of the field is stated in *Information Power*,[1] confirmed in Library Power,[2] and has been reiterated in the research literature. This is the basic premise underlying much of the school library media field, and is the basic philosophy behind the first school library media NBPTS portfolio entry.

HISTORY OF COLLABORATION

It is difficult to find exactly when the idea of partnering with classroom teachers to teach library and information skills first appeared in the school library media context. Certainly the idea of the school librarian as a teacher, requiring a strong teaching background and teaching skills, is present from the very beginning. Hannah Logasa in 1928 reflected the current thinking of the time, still relevant today, that the preparation of the school librarian should include training as both a teacher and as a librarian.[3] Althea Currin in 1939 encouraged the very best teachers in the school to consider gaining library school training in order to become school librarians.

The converse was also true, as Currin noted: "It may not be out of place to mention at this time the error of transferring teaching misfits to the school library field. A person who fails as a teacher probably lacks the very qualifications needed, either in personality or in background, to make a good school librarian."[4]

The concept of the school library media specialist as not just a teacher but an excellent teacher is one that started in the earliest phase of our profession.

BACKGROUND INFORMATION

As a field, we know that information skills are least effective when taught in isolation, with no immediate opportunity for students to apply those skills in the creation of a meaningful product. Those of us of a certain age well remember the information skills multiple-choice worksheets on using an encyclopedia index, the Dewey decimal system, and the card catalog. The skills learned in these lessons, which were developed to fill time in fixed-schedule classes, were lost before the class turned in their pencils and lined up at the door.

Information Power lists four major functions for the school library media specialist: teacher, information specialist, program administrator, and instructional partner. Collaboration is a major function of the teaching role, as well as an important philosophical basis for the instructional partner role. *Information Power* notes that "as instructional partner, the library media specialist joins with teachers and others to identify links across student information needs, curricular content, learning outcomes, and a wide variety of print, nonprint, and electronic information needs."[5]

Collaboration means working with a classroom teacher to co-plan the unit by weaving the information skills into the subject being taught; to co-teach the unit; and to co-assess student learning as a result of the project. These three parts, co-planning, co-teaching, and co-assessment, must all be part of the collaborative teaching unit.

Co-Planning

Co-planning means collaborating from the beginning. The classroom teacher has subject content responsibilities, proven strategies of teaching that content, and ideas for alternative methods. The library media specialist has information skills content responsibilities, proven strategies for teaching information skills, and alternative strategies as well. Together the classroom teacher and the library media specialist meld the collaborative unit. Plopping an information skill into a previously planned teacher content unit is not co-planning. Finding a teacher who will design a subject unit incorporating a favorite previously planned information skills lesson is not co-planning. If a library media specialist knows what information skills will be taught and the strategies that will be used to teach it, and is merely looking for a willing content teacher in which to embed the information skills, that is not co-planning.

Co-planning means meeting with a classroom teacher and discussing ways that the students can learn subject content and information skills. Co-planning starts from what John Dewey referred to as "suspended judgment," which occurs when the classroom teacher and the school library media specialist have only vague ideas. Dewey's definition of judgment as "the act of selecting and weighing the bearing of facts and suggestions as they present themselves, as well as of deciding whether the alleged facts are really facts and whether the idea used is a sound idea or merely passing fancy," applies to the scenario of the collaborative planning meeting, in which the school library media specialist and the classroom teacher suspend their judgment on how skills were previously taught in order to carefully consider new and possibly more effective strategies.[6] The time that this takes is important. Dewey also noted: "To many persons both suspense of judgment and intellectual search are disagreeable; they want to get them ended as soon as possible. They cultivate an over-positive and dogmatic habit of mind, or feel perhaps that a conduction of doubt will be regarded as evidence of mental inferiority."[7]

Co-planning means spending at least some time in organized planning sessions. A brief meeting in the hall is not sufficient for the level of planning required for true collaboration. These meetings can start at the curriculum development level at either the school or district level. Curricular collaboration can continue at building grade-level or department meetings, thus creating a pattern of increasingly more complex interactions. These interactions develop a sense of shared goals by classroom teachers and school library media specialists, culminating in the shared trust needed for true collaboration. This is achieved when both the classroom teacher and the school library media specialist willingly give of their time, seeing the planning process as crucial to teaching success.

After the first meeting or two when the collaborative process is beginning, e-mail communication can be used to continue the planning process, or to further hone the details of the collaborative unit. Candidates need to remember that the collaborative process is a win/win situation. The classroom teacher is not bestowing a gift on the school library media specialist, nor is the school library media specialist deigning to discuss content in an information skills lesson. This is a collaborative process. The school library media specialist needs to have as strong a role as the classroom teacher. If one role has to be stronger to make the unit work, it would be wise to ensure that it is the role of the school library media specialist. After all, the assessor spotlight will be looking closely at the library media side of the instruction.

Co-planning in the collaborative process cannot be forced, however. Withholding permission from a class to enter the library until proper forms have been filled out or planning meetings have been held is not only denying access to library services, but is also detrimental to the realization of the goals for the overall library program.

There are three kinds of power relationships.

Royalty/lowly subject. "If it pleases your majesty, may I, the lowly classroom teacher, bring my class to these hallowed halls?" In this relationship, the school library media specialist reigns supreme. Timid classroom teachers speak only when spoken to, and know that any request to use the library will be met with a stern glance and demands to know exactly for what purpose the space will be used. If that purpose is deemed worthy, permission may be granted. The drawbridge over the moat will be lowered, and the class may proceed into the library castle.

Professional/client. "I need to bring my class in. I was thinking about some time next week." The school library media specialist peers at the teacher, remembering the class behavior the last time this client entered, asks questions about the reasons, and sighs at the schedule to see when there is an opening. "I can see you next Tuesday at 2:00 p.m." The classroom teacher thinks about the problems caused by the rearranging of class time that will be necessary to make this work, but knows the futility of making other suggestions.

Friend-to-friend lunch date. Matching calendars, the school library media specialist and the classroom teacher pencil in, scribble, erase, discuss plans, and make it fit.

In both the royalty/subject and professional/client relationships, the school library media specialist clearly has the upper hand, is in charge of the process, and acts as the chatelaine of the castle, keys jangling at his or her belt. In the third example, by contrast, there is no power relationship. Instead there are two professionals, each with a clear sense of their worth to the learning process, who also appreciate the value of the other. Mutual trust is a hallmark of their collaboration.

Preparation for the co-planning session is important. If one is planning with seventh-grade social studies, it helps to be familiar with the curriculum in that subject area and in that grade level. Experienced library media specialists know to take a copy of the curriculum with them to the planning session, so that the information skills embedded in that curriculum can be readily identified. Over time, accomplished school library media specialists will know all of the subject and grade-level curricula as well as or better than they know the information skills curriculum, and in some cases will know the subject curricula better than the classroom teacher does. They know what is taught, and they also have a rough calendar in their head for when topics are taught, so that they can more easily slide information skills into the appropriate subject areas at the most conducive time.

The well-known analogy of the school library media specialist as wearing many hats is true, but the co-planning hat resembles a worn fishing hat complete with both often-used and unfamiliar lures of ideas gleaned from published units, information skills units, work with other classes, and adaptations from other sources.

Co-Teaching

Co-teaching and co-assessment can be interpreted that the classroom teacher and school library media specialist are joined at the hip, finishing each other's sentences and being in each other's presence during the whole of the unit. This is not necessarily true. Co-teaching certainly does not mean that the teacher and the library media specialist speak in tandem, or that they are even present during each other's teaching. However, the co-ness of the unit must be clearly established and evident in the design of the instruction. It is perfectly logical that the school library media specialist should take the lead in the teaching and assessment of information skills, and that the classroom teacher should take the lead in the teaching and assessment of the subject content. This should be decided jointly, however, and each part must be taught in context with the other.

Marilyn Friend and Lynne Cook list five strategies for co-teaching: assistive, support, parallel, alternative, and team teaching.[8]

Assistive teaching occurs when one teacher clearly has the main teaching role, and the other functions as an assistant. For integrated information skills instruction, this sometimes occurs at the beginning of the collaboration continuum, when the school library media specialist is just beginning to convince classroom teachers of the value of collaboration. The classroom teacher brings the class to the library media center, has control of content and time, and the library media specialist is in the helping role.

Support teaching is similar to assistive teaching. In support teaching, one teacher is working with students who need more direct assistance than other students. The student may need help with reading, with physical manipulation of resources, or have physical or emotional/behavioral limitations that require attention. In general, if students need this type of assistance, the support teacher will come to the library with the class, so that there may be three teaching professionals co-teaching the collaborative unit.

Parallel teaching divides the class by physical space. One teacher has part of the class, and another has a different group, but the instruction is the same for both groups. Rarely will this happen in the library media center. School library media specialists generally do not teach content skills. Although it is possible to do so at the elementary or middle school levels, very rarely are school library media specialists capable of teaching subjects such as advanced placement biology or honors French. The process of instruction should be the same regardless of school level. The classroom teacher has subject content; the school library media specialist has information skills content.

In *alternative teaching* situations, the class is divided by topic. The classroom teacher may keep part of the group in the classroom while the school library media specialist works with a group in the library; then the groups will switch. This is often used in the school library media program. It allows more individual attention to be given to each group, and maximizes the use of limited information resources.

Team teaching partners the school library media specialist and the classroom teacher. The two teachers work together to plan instruction. Although at any one time, one of them may have the main teaching role, the partners are comfortable adding to the instruction at any time. Students would have difficulty identifying which teacher was the main teacher. It's a team.

The type of co-teaching used is unimportant to the strength of the collaborative effort, but should be determined as part of the co-planning sessions. There may be good reasons for making decisions as to whether the whole class will be in the classroom, the school library media center, or in small groups scattered at various locations. The school library media specialist may choose to introduce the unit in the classroom, and the subject teacher may decide that it is logistically more reasonable to teach part of the content in the school library media center. Logistical details should flow from the design, but should not be structural barriers that affect the design.

Regardless of the method of co-teaching used, it will need to be obvious to the assessor that this is a co-taught unit. The purpose is collaboration. If it is not there, the result will be similar to a baking contest for chocolate chip cookies in which one of the entries does not contain chocolate chips.

Co-Assessment

In co-assessment, both the subject content and the information skills content must be assessed. Time available for instruction is precious, and the ability to maximize time on task is a factor in most evaluative processes for teachers. Can it be expected that precious learning time will be spent teaching skills if no one is checking to see if those skills have been learned? Even when the unit is literature-based and as simple as a storytelling, there is most likely a learning goal. Whatever it is, there should be a formal or an informal process to determine the learning progress of students.

The subject matter assessed in a collaborative project comprises subject content and information skills. Both are equally important. This does not mean that information skills needs to be a separate grade on the report card, or even a separate part of the unit, or that the library media specialist should be allocated grading responsibilities, although these could be the case. In the best collaborative units, information skills are woven so completely into the assignment and are such an integral part of each scoring guide and rubric that students or parents are not aware of the distinction between process and product.

Grant Wiggins and Jay McTighe, in their widely used book *Understanding by Design*, give rubrics for assessing student learning.[9] Many of their strategies for developing authentic assessment tools can be adapted to library media purposes, and will be good devices for taking to a collaborative co-planning session.

Assessment can be through the use of a written rubric or it can be through informal observation. Most likely the school library media specialist will use multiple ways to check the progress of student learning. Circulating among the class as they are working provides the school library media specialist with evidence of who may need more instruction, who is progressing nicely, and who may be completely lost. This very informal method of assessment should be documented by follow-up checklists besides the class roll. The next time the class enters, the school library media specialist can observe to see if progress has been made with specific information skills.

Asking the class to shout out answers or raise hands is not a valid method of assessment. The school library media specialist has no idea which students really know and which are merely going along with the group. Watching for verbal clues may help, but a true assessment method will provide evidence of the learning progress of each child.

A paper and pencil test on information skills is usually not a valid measure of progress either. A student may know all about an encyclopedia and answer every question correctly on a test, but still be unable to use the index. Authentic assessment measures learning progress by performing a task. Sitting in a library surrounded by the reality of books, databases, and other learning tools, one would have to wonder why the students are not assessed by their use of them.

STAGES OF COLLABORATION

There is a continuum of collaboration. It is unreasonable to think that every collaborative effort will result in that perfect stage of shared goals, shared trust, and shared responsibility that exemplifies collaboration at its highest level. It is more unreasonable still to think that strong collaborative efforts will appeal to all classroom teachers. The stages of collaboration can be thought of as a pathway. The road starts with *cooperation*, which can be as simple as basic communication, touching base, newsletters, and e-mail. It continues with *coordination*, which can be defined as putting forth effort to make either changes in pace or changes in content schedule in order to accommodate the learning happening in the classroom or in the library. True *collaboration*, though, is more than being aware of the instructional partner's curriculum, or being sensitive to a partner's instructional needs. True collaboration is valuing the partner area to the extent of changing one's own teaching.

Cooperation

Figure 5-1 describes cooperation by two hands touching. The library media specialist is cooperating with the classroom teacher to organize services or instruction of the library media program in order to match what is being taught in the classroom. The teacher is cooperating with the library media specialist by providing this information. The library media specialist usually instigates the cooperative effort, rather than the classroom teacher. In some cases, though, the classroom teacher may have been the first to approach, probably to ask for research time in the library, or for materials to assist with an upcoming unit.

FIGURE 5.1 ■ *Cooperation*

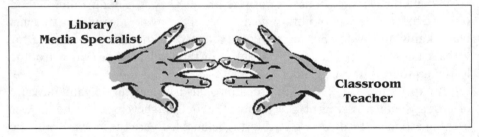

As this graphic also demonstrates, the real body of instruction occurs off the cooperative stage. Only the fingertips touch each other. This is cooperation. It does not require an emotional commitment, much if any trust, or even shared goals. Notes or e-mails, rather than face-to-face formal meetings, can be used for communication.

Providing information resources in the classroom or space in the library and assistance with individual reference questions is not an integrated unit of instruction. What if the teacher decided to wait a week? Since the library media specialist is in the supportive role, it doesn't matter. Even if the library media specialist provides a ten-minute introduction to library research at the beginning of the unit, even if the classroom teacher and library media specialist have met in the hall a few times to review what the students will do, this is still merely cooperating. If one hand is taken away from the graphic, the other hand is unchanged.

Cooperation is not a negative, however. Collaboration is a continuum, and cooperation may have to occur with some classroom teachers in order to take that important first step in building the level of trust required for true collaboration. Cooperation is important—but it is not collaboration.

Coordination

Now look at figure 5-2, which shows the two arms crossed. This figure represents the next stage of the continuum—coordination. The school library media specialist has made efforts to coordinate library instruction with what the classroom teacher is doing in the classroom.

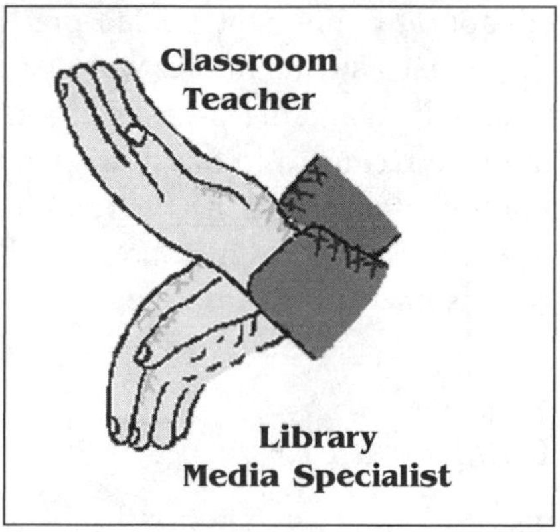

Perhaps the library media specialist will read a fiction story about a butterfly, since the class is currently studying butterflies. Or the isolated information skills class may be on proper bibliographic citation, since the class will be writing a research project in the next several weeks. The classroom teacher may incorporate information provided by the school library media specialist into classroom instruction, or in discussing an upcoming assignment may refer to skills the students have learned while in the library.

FIGURE 5.2 ■ *Coordination*

The school library media specialist is still, for the most part, in control of the coordinating effort. The library media specialist is making an effort to tie information skills instruction and library media center resources directly to current classroom content. The classroom teacher may or may not be doing the same. There is more communication required, but the territories of classroom and library still have well-defined turf boundaries.

In a typical coordination scenario, the school library media specialist has prepped the class by providing advance instruction in research skills. ("Next week, your teacher will be assigning . . . so we will go over what you will need to know today.") The teacher has scheduled work sessions for the class in the library. When they arrive, the library media specialist will most likely be available for individual help, and may provide a refresher to the introduction. It could be that the school library media specialist may decide to teach an information skill, perhaps bibliographic style, and may even volunteer or be asked to grade that part of the project.

This is still coordination, however. The bibliographic style grading is added to—tacked on at the end of—the *real* project. If the school library media specialist missed the opportunity to assist, there will always be another project. The library media specialist can always catch up with the classroom teacher at another time and plan to help with the next project. If the teacher is a week ahead or a week behind, it really doesn't matter. The unit can stand alone, though perhaps it requires the use of the library facilities and resources and may even require students to use previously learned information skills. But the design of the unit was not built with the information skills in mind. They are an add-on. This research unit depends on coordination, not collaboration.

Typically, the school library media specialist may find that students have retained little information learned in the previous lesson. Even though the students may do well, they have no reason to remember the information. Within a collaborative unit, the guided practice in using an encyclopedia index could be the actual assignment, but within a coordinated unit it is simply a precursor. The school library media specialist is steering his or her little red wagon of curriculum in one direction, and the classroom teacher is steering his or her little red wagon in another direction. It's wonderful that these roads are crossing, but if one gets to the crossroads a little late, or a little early, it really doesn't matter. The other road is unchanged. Coordination is important—but it is not collaboration.

Collaboration

The definition of a handshake is a good analogy for true collaboration. A handshake is defined clearly as two hands grasping each other. But picture figure 5-3 with the handshake broken apart. What is it now? The closest definition would be "not a handshake," or "two hands almost touching." The same is true of collaboration: it is made up of *co*-planning, *co*-teaching, and *co*-assessment of student learning. We may not be able to put a label on whatever the something else is—but it is *not* collaboration.

In collaborative projects, the design of the instruction and assessment is interwoven: both the classroom teacher and the school library media specialist have contributed to the design. Ideas, strategies, and content from both the classroom teacher and the library media specialist are reflected in the final project, as well as in how the unit will be taught and how it will be assessed. And further-

FIGURE 5.3 ■ *Collaboration*

more, both the classroom teacher and the school library media specialist are crucial to the success of the unit. If one is absent or falls behind, the unit will have to be redesigned.

INFORMATION SKILLS METHODOLOGIES

A harried elementary school supervisor, frustrated with a long day of training primary teachers to use new research-based techniques in the teaching of science, once remarked, "Sometimes I think that they really aren't teaching, they're just playing school." If school library media specialists are not collaborating with classroom teachers to teach information skills, and if they cannot discuss the instructional and research skills methodologies they are using, this description could be applied. They are not school library media specialists, they are just "playing library."

School library media specialists must be conversant with instructional methodologies such as constructivism, multiple intelligences, learning styles, and direct instruction in order to be part of the conversation around the instruction of students. The lexicon of these and other instructional methodologies, while rarely formalized in collaborative conversations, is still part of instructional development mental processes on the part of all educators.

School library media specialists must also be conversant with a range of information skills methodologies. The information skills area is one of the few in the school library media field in which a strong body of research exists to provide a sound research basis for instruction. School library media specialists should be familiar with the names of the leading thinkers in the area of information skills processing. This background knowledge provides the "why" for what we do.

Carol Kuhlthau is considered one of the strongest researchers in this area, and her publication of the Information Search Process (ISP) in 1993 has been updated by her latest work in which she deconstructs the search for information.[10] Other processes of interest to school library media specialists are Michael Eisenberg and Robert Berkowitz's Big6 information skills, which is probably the best known of all of the processes. The Big6 has an abridged version, the Super3, for younger students.[11] Big6 is a linear process and is fairly well structured. The best-known process that is less strict in its linear approach is Ken Macrorie's I-search.[12] Other information skills methodologies include Follett's Pathways to Knowledge and Barbara Stripling and Judy Pitts's mental models.[13]

School library media specialists may want to scan some of the further readings for this chapter, just to refresh their understanding of these theories. Classroom teachers may be unaware of these information skills methodologies. This is an opportunity for the school library media specialist to be at the center of positive change for the school by showing the value of an information skills process for classroom research.

PREPARING FOR THE COLLABORATION ENTRY

Accomplished teachers don't just deliver instruction. They are not content with being competent at playing school with a group of children. Accomplished teachers understand the science of pedagogy, the nature of learning, and know why and how they are teaching. For school library media specialists, this means being able to discuss Vygotsky's constructivism and Dewey's progressive education movement and how those theorists integrate with I-search versus Kuhlthau's ISP. For most library media specialists, this will involve a great deal of background reading in the theories underlying information skills instruction and inquiry learning.

The collaborative teaching of information skills is where school library media's twin professions of education and library or information science merge. The teaching of information skills requires a knowledge of the subject of information literacy, an understanding of the processes by which information skills are achieved, a modeling of that process in work with students and staff, and the ability to teach those skills to children. The school library media specialist is the information skills expert in the school and may be the only teacher with an understanding of information skills processes.

Even the most well-read school library media specialist will need to read background information from the field in order to be well-versed in the theory of collaboration. Marilyn Friend and Lynne Cook are considered the major authors in this field.[14]

In addition, there are several school library media writers that it would be helpful to read. Philip Turner and Ann Riedling's *Helping Teachers Teach* is an important benchmark regarding the instructional consultant role of the school library media specialist.[15] They stop short of the concept of the school library media specialist as teacher in the latest edition of their book, but it thoroughly covers the role of the school library media specialist in the instructional design process. Turner and Riedling's point that the school library has accepted all new responsibilities without deleting any is true and is an important point for reflection, but to some extent their assertion that the field has ambiguous roles has been resolved through the two editions of *Information Power*, the research of Library Power, and the nearly two decades of best practices that have evolved since the publication of the first edition of *Helping Teachers Teach* in 1988. The diversity in the field allows school library media specialists to capitalize on their personal strengths and professional interests. This allows school library media programs to vary to meet the varying needs of the school population, but the three roles set forth in *Information Power* and the responsibilities of the school library media specialist to act as a teacher of information skills are widely accepted.

In the 1980s the need to adapt to the new audiovisual and computer technology resources and services that could be offered did pose a problem, perhaps, but those roles have now been assimilated, and the ambiguous functions of instructional design and network specialists have evolved into separate positions. It is true that the school librarian sometimes has to assist with those other duties, but usually they are not considered part of the education, training, or job description of the school librarian.

David Loertscher's taxonomy of school library services is another hallmark of collaboration. Loertscher's concept of the school library continuum as moving from the self-help warehouse, in which no interaction occurs between the school library media specialist and the classroom teacher, to increasingly more complex instructional interactions, in which the school librarian is involved in the curriculum planning function, is a good vehicle for reflection about the library program. Loertscher's taxonomies can be easily adapted to use as evaluation instruments regarding the school library media program.[16]

For other readings, see the "Further Reading" section at the end of chapter 3. Candidates may want to keep copies of some of the major books at hand. It can be comforting to refer back to Turner or Loertscher in the late-night writing frenzy and see the parallels between the ideals of good library practice and the reality of accomplished teaching in school library media. Stripling and Hughes-Hassell's *Curriculum Connections through the Library* will be especially useful.[17]

Collaborative teaching starts with one person at a time. For the collaboration entry, candidates do not need to be collaborating with every teacher in the school. They need just one teacher, for one unit, at one point in time. Of course, after one teacher collaborates successfully, then another teacher at the same grade level wants the same type of attention, then other grade levels get interested, and soon the school slides down the muddy hill into the collaborative environment you were trying to get to in the first place. It starts with one teacher at a time.

Sometimes the classroom teacher's style takes precedence in the collaborative teaching of information skills. Real collaboration occurs when both the classroom teacher and the school library media specialist have enough trust to break out of the direct instruction drill and practice worksheets to try a constructivist project using I-search. Most important, though, is for the school library media candidate to be able to discuss instructional methodologies and research methodologies in reflection. Otherwise, we really are just "playing library."

Food for Thought

Use Loertscher's taxonomy to evaluate your school library program. Where do classroom teachers, administrators, or support staff see the role of your library? Think of the classroom teachers in your school. Divide them into cooperators, coordinators, and collaborators. Write about your experiences with each of them. Are there times when you have successfully moved a teacher up the continuum? How did that happen?

Try the same project using different information skills processes. What happens when Big6 is used compared with I-search? Are there differences between linear-thinking children and those who need a less-structured approach? This is a great opportunity to write about the learning of individual students.

Identify several teachers whom you could approach for an NBPTS collaboration entry. Begin conversations with them about possible collaborative ventures. It's best if your first collaborative venture is not your NBPTS entry. Practice!

NOTES

1. American Association of School Librarians, Association for Educational Communications and Technology, *Information Power: Building Partnerships for Learning* (Chicago: American Library Association, 1998). See the specific information on the teaching and learning role of the school library media specialist.
2. Library Power was a massive grant program funded by the Reader's Digest Dewitt Wallace Foundation. The funds poured money into local education foundations for the purpose of improving school libraries. For an overview and evaluation of Library Power, see Douglas Zweizig and Dianne McAfee Hopkins, *Lessons from Library Power: Enriching Teaching and Learning* (Englewood, CO: Libraries Unlimited, 2000).
3. Hannah Logasa, *The High School Library: Its Function in Education* (New York: Appleton, 1928).
4. Althea M. Currin, *School Library Management*, 6th ed. (New York: H. W. Wilson, 1939).

5. *Information Power*, 4. For a more thorough examination of this role, see Betty P. Cleaver and William D. Taylor, *The Instructional Consultant Role of the School Library Media Specialist* (Chicago: American Library Association, 1989).

6. John Dewey, *How We Think: A Restatement of the Relation of Reflective Thinking to the Educative Process* (Boston: Heath, 1933), 12.

7. Dewey, *How We Think*, 131.

8. Marilyn Friend and Lynne Cook, *Integration* (White Plains, NY: Longmans, 1993).

9. Grant P. Wiggins and Jay McTighe, *Understanding by Design* (Alexandria, VA: Association for Supervision and Curriculum Development, 1998). See especially the chart on p. 64 for a good overview of the backward design process.

10. Carol Collier Kuhlthau, *Seeking Meaning: A Process Approach to Library and Information Services*, 2nd ed. (Westport, CT: Libraries Unlimited, 2004).

11. For a complete overview of the Big6 process, visit thehttp://www.big6.org site. See also Michael B. Eisenberg and Robert E. Berkowitz, *Curriculum Initiative: An Agenda and Strategy for Library Media Programs* (Worthington, OH: Linworth, 1988).

12. Ken Macrorie, *The I-Search Paper* (Portsmouth, NH: Boynton/Cook, 1988).

13. For more information, see Barbara K. Stripling and Judy M. Pitts, *Brainstorms and Blueprints: Teaching Library Research as a Thinking Process* (Englewood, CO: Libraries Unlimited, 1988); and Marjorie L. Pappas and Ann E. Tepe, *Pathways to Knowledge and Inquiry Learning* (Greenwood Village, CO: Libraries Unlimited, 2002).

14. Friend and Cook, *Integration*.

15. Philip M. Turner and Ann Marlow Riedling, *Helping Teachers Teach: A School Library Media Specialist's Role*, 3rd ed. (Westport, CT: Libraries Unlimited, 2003).

16. David V. Loertscher, *Taxonomies of the School Library Media Program*, 2nd ed. (San Jose, CA: Hi Willow, 2000).

17. Barbara Stripling and Sandra Hughes-Hassell, eds., *Curriculum Connections through the Library* (Westport, CT: Libraries Unlimited, 2003).

6 Encouraging Literature Appreciation

The encouragement of reading, which can be loosely defined as helping children and youth to develop the lifelong habit of reading, has been a hallmark of the school library media profession from the very beginning. In 1957 S. R. Ranganathan's five laws of library science, shown in figure 6-1, gave the basis for the act of reading as a major emphasis in the library science profession.[1]

Ranganathan's laws outline the basic principles underlying the encouragement of reading and are still applicable today. Providing open access to books and information in all formats and providing readers with a rich variety of reading materials from which to choose are the basic premises underlying librarianship. Many school library media specialists would note today that the draw for them in entering the profession was the joy they received from matching a child with the perfect book. That joy continues for most school library media specialists, along with the joy of seeing a middle schooler excited over finding exactly the right information for a research paper, or a high schooler exclaiming over finding updated sports scores.

The *Information Power* mission of ensuring that students and staff are effective users of ideas and information and the role of informa-

FIGURE 6-1 ■ *Ranganathan's Five Laws of Library Science*

1. Books are for use	4. Save the time of the reader
2. Every reader his book	5. The library is a growing organism
3. Every book its reader	

tion access and delivery in general are still as valid today as when ideas and information were contained only in print hardcover books.[2]

The role of literature appreciation in English/language arts and perhaps other subject areas in education goes beyond simply wanting children and young people to read by encouraging them to understand the literary aspects of the written word. Literature appreciation for the school library media profession tends to center on the love of literature as a pleasurable activity rather than on the technical aspects of literature.

By integrating these two concepts of literature appreciation, however, school library media specialists can encourage readers to be selective in their choice of reading materials in print and electronic formats and in their choice of videos and sound recordings. School library media specialists want children to understand and articulate their reading preferences, to talk about the books they read, and to understand why reading those books was a satisfying experience.

When libraries were first placed in schools in the mid-nineteenth century, their primary purpose was focused on reading. Reading, even in that stage, was seen as a crucial part of the educational experience.[3]

Reading is a part of the advocacy movement in libraries today. The slogan "Kids Who Read, Succeed," used in the past by the American Library Association, is still interpreted to mean that reading is the most important link to academic achievement, and remains a hallmark of the library profession.[4]

The encouragement of reading remains a major reason why school library media specialists enter the profession. That traditional focus continues, but the emphasis on connecting children with books has now grown to encompass the entire world of information resources. Reading print in general, and reading fiction specifically, is still a focus in the library world, but the emphasis on reading print fiction has been joined by an emphasis on reading, listening, viewing, and otherwise sharing in the whole range of print, electronic, and nonprint resources that are available today.

THE HISTORY OF LITERATURE AND SCHOOL LIBRARIES

The encouragement of reading was one of the foundations on which the school library media field was built. Henry Cecil and Willard Heaps in 1940 noted that the functions of a school library were to enrich classroom instruction, encourage reading, stimulate the appreciation of literature, encourage individual progress through reading, and teach the use of books.[5] This formative definition gives a sense of the richness in the use of literature and sets the stage for a modern definition that is not bounded by simply reading fiction for pleasure.

Most library historians note that school libraries began for three reasons. First, changes in teaching strategies in the mid-nineteenth century encouraged the use of materials in classroom instruction that could supplement the use of textbooks. Second, teachers moved away from the recitation as an instructional exercise, which was little more than a dry regurgitation of facts, to a more project-based form of teaching. This coincided with the progressive movement of John Dewey.[6] This move to what would become inquiry learning required resources other than texts, such as encyclopedias and other reference books, as well as nonfiction. And third, during this era, reading for mental stimulation was encouraged for all facets of the community. The use of lectures, public libraries, and reading circles to improve the mind was seen as crucial to society and was established for people of all ages.

The call for a library to be placed in every school and the gaining of permission to use tax dollars earmarked for schools in the construction, staffing, and equipping of school libraries were important steps in creating the lifelong habit of self-improvement through reading.

Money for library books in the early days was based on a matching funds concept. In Danville, Virginia, for instance, if a school librarian raised fifteen dollars, it was matched by the school district, and this total was matched again by the state department of education. Therefore, for every fifteen dollars raised, the school librarian would have sixty dollars to spend.[7] Most school libraries were stocked in this fashion, which is far from the per-pupil method used today. The purchase of books, however, was closely restricted. It was noted by one superintendent that the books purchased would not be frivolous ones, but rather classics that would further the mind of the reader. Azile Wofford noted that in New York state in 1892, Melvil Dewey was instrumental in the passage of a law that "designated the school library as a part of school equipment with space in the school building, and required that it provide books for reference work, recreational reading for pupils, and professional books for teachers."[8]

Some states furthered the restrictions on reading by the use of a standard book list from which books would be chosen for the school library. The books to be purchased were mandated in some states, but in others were merely strongly encouraged. In Virginia, for instance, books on the state list were deeply discounted, whereas books not on the list were available, but at the standard price. This occurred in spite of a consensus that the selection of library materials was the prime responsibility of the school librarian.

BACKGROUND AND OVERVIEW

The function of literature appreciation in school library media settings can be separated into the following parts: a knowledge of books and other resources for children and youth; a knowledge of the use of books and other resources in the curriculum; the articulation of the importance of reading strategies and skills; and the teaching of literature appreciation through interaction.

Knowledge of Books and Other Resources

The field of materials for children and youth is based on a proud history of excellence in writing and illustration. Knowledge of this field depends on two areas. The first is knowledge of the criteria used in the selection of resources, and the second is familiarity with known works of quality. The courses in children's and young adult resources in school library preparation programs tend to vary in their approach. Some children's literature courses are taught as a survey literature course, reviewing the major works and genres. Others are taught with the goal of teaching the criteria and selection for excellence in children's writing. Although each of these approaches has merit, it may mean that the NBPTS candidate will need to feel highly skilled in both areas. Common texts used in children's and young adult literature coursework are Lukens's *Critical Handbook of Children's Literature* and Nilsen and Donelson's *Literature for Today's Young Adults.*[9]

In general, the standard selection criteria of authoritativeness, relevance to the curriculum, literary merit, appropriateness, and other criteria apply to all types of resources. But beyond those, other criteria specific to the literature genre also apply. Candidates may want to review recent texts on this topic in order to feel confident when applying selection criteria to, for example, alphabet picture books.

It is expected that accomplished school library media specialists will be familiar with most of the widely identified works of literary quality. The Association for Library Service to Children (ALSC) and the Young Adult Library Services Association (YALSA), both divisions of the American Library Association, present most of the major awards for resources for children and youth.[10] These associations distinguish children's books as being for children from birth through age 14, and young adult books as being for young people of ages 10–18. This overlap causes some confusion, as some of the books on the cusp of each age group may be selected for awards in either group. Figure 6-2 lists the major awards for children and youth.

Of the awards, the Newbery Medal, given for the writing of books for youth, and the Caldecott Medal, given for the illustration of children's books,

FIGURE 6-2 ■ *Major Awards for Children's and Young Adult Literature*

AWARD	AWARDED BY
Caldecott Medal	ALSC
Newbery Medal	ALSC
Pura Belpré Medal	ALSC
Coretta Scott King Award	ALSC
Robert Sibert Medal	ALSC
ALEX Award	YALSA
Best Books for Young Adults	YALSA
Michael Printz Award	YALSA

are considered the most prestigious ones and are sometimes described as the "Oscars" for children's and young adult literature.

Using Books and Other Resources in the Curriculum

The visual image of a story being read to children often overlooks the importance of that story's link to the curriculum. Even stories selected for pure enjoyment should have a reason for their selection. In some cases, that reason is tied to classroom content, such as reading Polacco's *Pink and Say* to coincide with classroom study of the Civil War, or Judi Barrett's *Cloudy with a Chance of Meatballs* for a unit on weather study.[11] In other cases, the story may be selected based on a literature theme, author study, or type of material. Regardless, the reason for choosing a particular resource at a particular time must be clearly articulated, even if the reason is simply that of introducing children to literature of various genres or types of stories.

In the highest level of literature appreciation, the planning of the literature activity is an identical process to that of collaboration. The school library media specialist collaborates with classroom teachers to plan the literature to be used for storytimes, for parallel reading, or perhaps as supplementary texts for class projects. The classroom teacher and the school library media specialist decide which of them will read specific literature works, whether it be the library media specialist in the library, the classroom teacher in the classroom, or both together in constructing a follow-up literature activity. Although co-assessment may seem awkward in literature appreciation, student learning progress in the encouragement of reading can still be assessed, at least informally. The literature selected for use teaches, enriches, or furthers a concept in the content area or grade level, and is reinforced by activities conducted in either the library or the classroom.

Articulating Reading Strategies and Skills

In some states, courses in the teaching of reading are required as part of the school library media certification program. The rationale for this is an important one: that the teaching of reading has changed dramatically since undergraduate teacher education, and school library media specialists must be able to participate in school-level conversations about reading. Decisions made about reading have a direct connection to the use of literature in the library program.

The controversy over the best way to teach reading, often referred to as the "reading wars," is also crucial for school librarians to understand. It is best not to take sides in this passionate debate, but rather to be able to work effectively with classroom teachers of any reading mind-set. Several issues of *Phi Delta Kappan* shed light on a debate over reading that at times has been quite contentious, as researchers on the importance of phonic understanding and those on the side of a more whole-word approach have written articles, letters to the editors, and other commentary.[12] The extreme of this approach is to use library media specialist time in the teaching of reading strategies, rather than encouraging reading in its broadest form. Candidates in school districts or states under this mandate will need to plan carefully to develop activities that are more in line with best practice in the field.

Accelerated Reader and other electronic reading programs also figure into this debate. In these programs, books are assigned reading levels. Students are tested for their level, read books, and then take computerized tests of basic recall. Points are awarded for the difficulty of the book. In some schools, the points can be used to buy trinkets, or even larger prizes. The points are also used for grading purposes at times.

Betty Carter was one of the first to criticize electronic reading programs in her landmark article "Hold the Applause!" published in 1996 in *School Library Journal*.[13] Carter's article and subsequent letters to the editor from school library media specialists weighed in on both sides of the electronic reading program debate. Some school library media specialists decried the emphasis placed on these programs and despaired of encouraging children to read a wide variety of literature that might not be covered by a reading test. Other library media specialists applauded the new electronic reading programs, noting that they saw children eagerly reading who had not been moved by any previous reading initiative.

Stephen Krashen is also outspokenly opposed to these programs, noting that they can actually discourage reading. Krashen's *The Power of Reading* in 1993 first outlined his concept of free voluntary reading (FVR) and its importance in the educational process. Since then, Krashen has published a new edition of *The Power of Reading* and has continued to advocate strongly for FVR through columns, articles, editorials, and letters to the editors commenting on news stories about reading issues.[14]

The debate continues about electronic reading programs. School library media specialists are encouraged to see children reading, but are concerned about the resources used to buy computers and tests. At times classroom teachers refuse to allow students to check out books that are not on the list, or for which no tests have been developed. Although the programs have improved the range of literature, they are still geared more toward fiction reading than nonfiction.

Candidates must weigh the dangers of highlighting a program on which clear and passionate sides have been taken. Although engagement in all educational processes in the school is certainly important, it may be wise to place any specific reading program in the context of the school, and perhaps note clearly that the candidate's specific strategy is only one of several that are used to encourage reading.

Literature through Interactive Discussions

"Wasn't that a good story? Okay, it's time to check out books now" will not produce a high score on the literature appreciation entry for NBPTS. Interaction regarding the work of literature, either among students or between students and teacher, is required. This is not something that always occurs in the school library media center, especially at the high school and middle school levels. The rationale for interaction, however, goes back to encouraging reading as a lifelong habit. If this role is truly accepted, then it is crucial to know how students react to a variety of literary plots, themes, and genres.

School library media specialists use many strategies to engage students in literature, and some of these may be indirect. Displays, face-front bookstore shelving, and other strategies encourage students to read and check out materials. The practitioner literature has many articles that discuss displays, interactive activities, and collaborative strategies to encourage reading.[15]

RESEARCH IN LITERATURE APPRECIATION

By far the best source for an overview of writings on young adult literature is Richard Abrahamson's "Collected Wisdom: The Best Articles Ever Written on Young Adult Literature and Teen Reading." In this short article, Abrahamson profiles twenty-five journal articles, from 1912 to 1995, that review the rationale and give an overview of the field, including books used in the classroom and censorship issues.[16]

Noted researchers in the library media field are Stephen Krashen for his *Power of Reading* and the texts of Lukens and Nilsen and Donelson, as noted previously. School library media specialists preparing for the literature appreciation entry should also become familiar with the materials published by the International Reading Association, the ALSC, and YALSA. The reviews of materials that are available on the websites of these associations can provide an overview, as well as access to information on current issues.[17]

SUMMARY

The encouragement of reading goes beyond the selection and promotion of good reading, although that is certainly important. Advocating for specific books through the use of book displays, book contests and promotions, and personally advocating by literally placing a book in a child's hands are also important, but the field has matured past these concepts.

The literature appreciation entry is discussed further in chapter 10, but in preparing for this entry, candidates will need a sound background in selecting literature in its broadest definition for children and youth, integrating that literature into classroom content, understanding the context of reading in schools, and specific strategies for interacting with children and youth regarding literature.

Food for Thought

What sells in a book display? Sometimes we display new books, or even pull random books to display on top of the shelves to entice reading. However, if libraries were bookstores, displays would be evaluated to see which ones attracted buyers. Make your own marketing analysis. Thoughtfully pull books to entice readers, and analyze what happens. Ask students why they chose a particular book. Reflect on the relationship between children and youth and their reading.

Work with a classroom teacher to have students journal about their reading. Give prompts about the book they liked the least or the best; or ask what they look for when they reach for a book.

Begin reading books for age levels different from those in your school. Annotate the bibliography, and then reflect on ways that literature can be used in the curriculum.

NOTES

1. S. R. Ranganathan, *The Five Laws of Library Science* (New York: Asia, 1963).

2. American Association of School Librarians, Association for Educational Communications and Technology, *Information Power: Building Partnerships for Learning* (Chicago: American Library Association, 1998).

3. Martha Wilson, comp., *Selected Articles on School Library Experience*, 2nd ed. (New York: H. W. Wilson, 1932).

4. "Kids Who Read, Succeed," was a slogan from the American Library Association. More information about the ALA's advocacy program can be found at http://www .ala.org/ala/issues/issuesadvocacy.htm.

5. Henry A. Cecil and Willard A. Heaps, *School Library Service in the United States: An Interpretative Survey* (New York: H. W. Wilson, 1940).

6. John Dewey was one of the foremost educational philosophers in the area of inquiry learning. His works, many of which are in the public domain, are frequently used as the basis of constructivism. Some of his important works are *Democracy and Education* (New York: Macmillan, 1916), *Experience and Education* (New York: Macmillan, 1938), and *How We Think* (New York: Heath, 1933).

7. Mary Virginia Gaver, *A Braided Cord: Memoirs of a School Librarian* (Metuchen, NJ: Scarecrow, 1988).

8. Azile Wofford, "School Library Evolution," *Phi Delta Kappan* 22 (February 1940): 285–88.

9. The latest editions of these works are Rebecca J. Lukens, *A Critical Handbook of Children's Literature*, 7th ed. (Boston: Pearson, 1997); and Alleen Pace Nilsen and Kenneth L. Donelson, *Literature for Today's Young Adults*, 7th ed. (Boston: Pearson, 2004).

10. A complete list of the award-winning resources, along with the criteria used to identify them, can be found on the websites of the ALSC (http://www.ala.org/alsc) and YALSA (http://www.ala.org/yalsa).

11. Patricia Polacco, *Pink and Say* (New York: Philomel Books, 1998); Judi Barrett, *Cloudy with a Chance of Meatballs* (New York: Atheneum, 1978).

12. Specific articles of interest are Joanne Yatvin, "Babes in the Woods: The Wanderings of the National Reading Panel," *Phi Delta Kappan* 83, no. 5 (January 2002): 364–69; and Richard L. Allington, "What I've Learned about Effective Reading Instruction from a Decade of Studying Exemplary Elementary Classroom Teachers," *Phi Delta Kappan* 83, no. 10 (June 2002): 740–47.

13. Betty Carter, "Hold the Applause! Do Accelerated Reader and Electronic Bookshelf Send the Right Message?" *School Library Journal* 42 (October 1996): 22–26.

14. Stephen Krashen, *The Power of Reading* (Englewood, CO: Libraries Unlimited, 1993). Krashen's latest edition of this work is now available as well (Englewood, CO: Libraries Unlimited, 2005). For more information on Stephen Krashen's writing, visit his website at http://www.sdkrashen.com/main.php3.

15. Richard F. Abrahamson, "Collected Wisdom: The Best Articles Ever Written on Young Adult Literature and Teen Reading," *English Journal* 86, no. 3 (March 1997): 50–54.

16. Some practitioner journals of interest in this area are *Book Links, Library Media Connection, School Library Media Activities Monthly*, and *School Library Journal*, to name a few.

17. The association websites are as follows:

    International Reading Association (http://www.ira.org),
    Association for Library Service to Children (http://www.ala.org/alsc), and
    Young Adult Library Services Association (http://www.ala.org/yalsa).

7 Integration of Technology

David Loertscher noted that when audiovisual technologies first entered the library program, it was an integration of format.[1] Computer and Internet technologies became an integration of content. This distinction is only partially true. Audiovisual materials, for the most part, were never fully integrated into the collection. Even today in most school libraries, audiovisual materials are kept in a separate room, sometimes even under lock and key. Their use is restricted to teachers, and sometimes to teachers of specific grade levels. Students who are accustomed to using videos in every other aspect of their lives are denied access to them for instructional purposes.

Imagine that same attitude with books. "No, I'm sorry, you can't read *Charlotte's Web* because your teacher will read it to you next year." In truth, much of the reason for this situation has to do with the misuse of audiovisual materials in the educational process. Videos are shown as an enrichment or reward after the topic is fully taught, with lights off, and at the end of the day, or even at the end of the week. The use of video as a teaching device, with note-taking expected as part of content delivery, rarely occurs. If it did, it would not matter if students had seen the video before, and it would be viewed as a positive if they had. The reiteration of important facts is generally considered to be a positive in the educational process, not a negative.

The unfortunate fact is that audiovisual resources are still seen in many schools as a reward for behavior, as a break for the teacher, or as a summary or enrichment, not as an active teaching tool. In addition, not all school library media specialists actively embraced audiovisual materials when they first entered libraries, which may explain why there was an attempt to "keep them in their place," which in the case of most such materials meant they were locked in the back room, waiting for one teacher to arrive at the one space in the textbook where the one video, film, or filmstrip would be used. Contrast this use with that of the same information contained in print books, which are checked out to students for serendipitous learning throughout the school year.

Electronic technologies have fared little better. They have for the most part managed to make their way into the main library room, but are usually clustered together in specific places. The predominant visual image is that of separateness: of a physical distinction between electronic resources and print ones. The use of filters that restrict some of the most pertinent content, restrictions on student e-mail and chat, and prohibitions on serendipitous Internet browsing have further limited the impact of electronic technology in schools. Turn your back on the computer area and the library will look the same as it did in 1950. In some of our most underfunded libraries this is unfortunately the literal truth, even when looking closely at the shelves.

Technology is regarded differently from print in its use as well. "Print first" is a watchword in many school library media center research projects. This places the nature of the medium at a higher level of importance than the information contained in it. The required use of one medium before another regardless of relevancy of content is always suspect. Some uses are best met by print resources such as almanacs, full-length print books, or journal articles. Some uses are best met by electronic resources, and still others by audiovisual resources.

Information is the product that school library media specialists offer their customers. That said, the containers in which the information is housed, and the conduits through which we access that information, are also of interest to school library media specialists. Although network administration, webmastering, and other advanced technology specialties are only tangential to the school library field, sometimes the school library media specialist has the ability to act in these roles. The school library media specialist will often learn the skills needed to perform limited functions in each of these job roles. In any case, the hardware, software, connectivity, and use of information technologies are important concepts in the school library media field.

BACKGROUND AND OVERVIEW

Over the years, the school library media specialist has gone from being a keeper of the books to presiding over a multimedia center. Not too many decades ago, a required course in school library media preparation was the audiovisual course, where prospective classroom teachers and school library media specialists labored to use dry mount presses and slide sorters and learned to thread 16-mm film projectors.

Today's information technology is not so easily stored in the back room, however. School library media specialists, along with other librarians in public, university, and special library settings, have to make decisions on how to integrate electronic information resources, electronic program administration systems, and the equipment needed to make everything work. In the early 1980s, when CD-ROMs and controlled vocabularies first began to appear, very few had a true glimpse of what the future held. Librarians attended workshops in which an entire encyclopedia was shown stored on a single compact disc. We watched salesmen toss videodiscs into the air because they were unbreakable, only to be told just a few years later that wiping them with a tissue might wipe the data from them.

After the initial hoopla over the "bells and whistles" of digitized information, selection principles began to be applied to electronic technology. Gail Dickinson's *Selection and Evaluation of Electronic Resources*, along with Pam Berger and Susan Kinnell's *CD-ROM for Schools*, appeared to help move the selection choices from what the technology could do to what information the technology could deliver.[2]

New peripheral devices and storage formats appeared on the horizon constantly, and new electronic resources were developed to maximize the expanding capabilities of ever more powerful computers. CD-ROMs were attached externally, then computers were developed with internal CD drives, which then moved to CD/DVD formats. The computer labs built in schools were constantly seen as out-of-date, and decisions to invest thousands of dollars in technology were seen as unavoidable.

The automation of school library circulation and catalog systems occurred at a time when school libraries were at their lowest funding point. Thousands of dollars were poured into computers, software, and the physical bar coding required for automation. School library media specialists were forced to learn about MARC records, standardization of subject headings, and other areas of specialized technical services. School library media specialists had to become both skilled users and skilled managers of technology, both for informational and for library administrative purposes.

TECHNOLOGY AND NBPTS

In some ways, the field of information technology has matured to the point of being institutionalized. Computer hardware has been standardized to some extent, so that most new computers in libraries can function at the level required by most of the resources. Decisions of whether to have computer labs, to distribute the networks to the classrooms, or to do both are made with a growing sense of confidence in the capabilities of electronic information resources and technologies and how they will be used in the classroom.

The school library media specialist must be at the center of those decisions. Although more and more schools are hiring technology facilitators to make the networks and servers function, the school library media specialist as the information skills and information resources expert must be involved with the technology.

Preparation for this role is sketchy. Although most school library preparation programs include coursework in technology, it may not be sufficient at the level required for a new school library media specialist to act as a network administrator. Additional learning is still partly based on aptitude or previous experience.

Much of the writing in technology is very specific as well. In the other areas covered by the NBPTS principles, specific authors or seminal works can be pointed to as essential. That is only somewhat true for the area of technology, since much will depend on the school library media specialist's self-assessment of his or her skills, knowledge, and experience in this area.

Figure 7-1 illustrates one possible way to approach technology in preparation for the NBPTS process. At the top, first and foremost, are information resources, which include but are not limited to Internet resources, controlled

FIGURE 7-1 ■ *The I-H-C Pyramid*

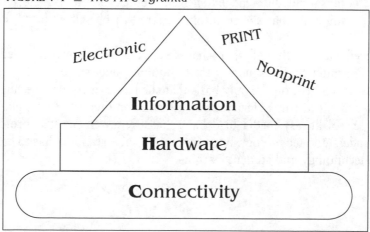

vocabulary databases, other instructional software used in the school, and the range of audiovisual resources. Also included as information resources are services little used in schools but often used by students, such as chat, virtual communities, and even e-mail.

Supporting the information resources is the hardware used in schools, i.e., computers and peripherals and audiovisual equipment. The hardware is chosen to support the information resources or services, not the reverse. New gadgets are only useful in education to the extent to which there is an instructional or information use for them.

Supporting all of these are the electronic systems that connect the hardware and information resources to the user. This category certainly includes systems and networks, but it also includes policies and procedures. In some schools, instant messaging is available to help students with homework; and teachers and students, even those in the elementary grades, can e-mail back and forth. In other schools, any type of e-mail is forbidden, and teachers are not allowed to use the school network to check their e-mail for messages from parents or to do their graduate coursework. The digital divide exists not in our hardware so much as in our policies.

Information resources, hardware, and support systems must exist in the framework of student learning. Student learning is the purpose of education, and educational technology must be embedded in the student learning framework.

The extent to which NBPTS candidates have grown up with or used technology will make a difference in this entry. Candidates who use a wide range of technology in their personal and professional lives may be able to scan the literature and immediately feel confident in their knowledge and skills. Other candidates may read the literature without understanding it. A school library colleague once remarked to me that she did not consider herself to be computer illiterate, because she did read extensively about computers; she just didn't understand anything that she read. She referred to herself as just "computer-dumb."

I argued with her, though, that what she did understand was the needs of students and learning. She was judging the technology, since she did not truly understand how it worked, on the only basis that she had, which was the impact that it had on student learning. That is truly information literacy at its highest level.

The school library media field has a basic requirement that professionals need to understand technology, but our greatest understanding has to be the link between technology and student learning.

SUMMARY

School libraries sometimes physically look as if the field has desperately tried to keep technology as far away from print resources as possible. We do not allow information contained within technology to reside in the neighborhood of books, we sometimes force students to use print first, and we create structures in which the use of information contained in technological media is severely constrained.

This may be a hurdle for some candidates. The best way to prepare for technology with NBPTS is to consider the ways in which it is allowed to positively impact student learning, and to have a basic understanding of how technology is integrated into the instructional lives of students through information resources, through hardware, and through the systems designed to support their use.

Food for Thought

How much technology do you use on a daily basis? Keep an information journal, and for one day write down every interaction that you have when you receive or share information. Your list may include television, e-mail, radio, and personal communication, along with print sources such as newspapers or books. Now ask your students to do the same. Are we teaching students to make good choices about the different information media?

The best preparation to learn about the systems that support technology may be to look over the shoulders of technicians as they work. Ask questions, and begin to write down your reflections about the answers you receive.

Make your personal use of technology as wide as possible. Begin using services such as instant messaging, and ask your students about websites they are using. Many of these sites are positive, and you may find your understanding of technology to be broadened tremendously.

NOTES

1. David V. Loertscher, *Taxonomies of the School Library Media Program*, 2nd ed. (San Jose, CA: Hi Willow, 2000).
2. Gail K. Dickinson, *Selection and Evaluation of Electronic Resources* (Littleton, CO: Libraries Unlimited, 1994). See also Pam Berger and Susan Kinnell, *CD-ROM for Schools: A Directory and Practical Handbook for Media Specialists* (Wilton, CT: Eightbit Books, 1994).

8 Other Best Practices

A book on school library media best practices would be extremely comprehensive and would probably end up as a multivolume set. In the 1960s, as part of the Knapp School Library Manpower Project, the *Behavioral Requirements Analysis Checklist* listed over 700 tasks performed by school library media professionals.[1] Although most of the tasks listed then are still valid today, the areas in which school library media specialists are expected to function have grown tremendously.

The major performance areas that have been discussed so far in part 2 are collaborating to teach information skills, encouraging literacy, and integrating technology. This chapter will briefly discuss several other best practices current to the school library media field. Rather than relating to specific NBPTS entries, the best practices in this chapter will be useful to candidates in all areas of the NBPTS process.

ADVOCACY

"Kids Who Read, Succeed." "@ your library."[2] These slogans, which are still used in the library field, reflect advocacy campaigns designed to change the image of libraries in the mind of the public. The need to inform the public about libraries has always been important. It seems that as soon as libraries began, there also arose a need to change their image in the public's mind. Early readings show this quite clearly. In the 1980s this movement changed from public relations to that of marketing. In the 1990s the term of choice was *advocacy*.

Definition

Advocacy is partly public relations and partly marketing, and yet it is neither of these two terms. Public relations implies a one-way focused message that is designed to advance a certain part of the library's programs—perhaps its speaker program, or children's storytelling. It can also be used to advance a specific agenda, such as a library card campaign or a library book club. Public relations' one-way message tells the library's story: who it is, what it does, and how it does it. The term *public relations* implies the way the library is perceived by the public, to make sure that the correct message is received.

Marketing implies selling. In marketing, the library has a product, service, or event to sell to the public. The public has to be made aware not only that it needs the product or service, but that the library's specific product is the one to best meet that need. Marketing has a transaction as its goal.

Advocacy, on the other hand, is more than either public relations or marketing. Advocacy is based on mission and beliefs and is a "planned coordinated continuum of efforts to advance the library program, shared with a developed community of supporters, and based on a broad, definable goal." It is a "planned, deliberate, and sustained effort to raise awareness of an issue or issues."[3]

Gary Hartzell presaged the advocacy movement with his publication of "The Invisible School Librarian" in 1997. This article made several key points.

- The school library field is conceptually mature.
- Invisibility is the problem, not enmity.
- Good school library programs create their own support.
- The school library media profession is based on education best practices.[4]

These four points are key to the understanding of advocacy in the school library media field. The maturity of the school library media field began with the 1986 publication of *Information Power* and continued with Library Power and the 1998 edition of *Information Power*.[5] We know what good school library media specialists are supposed to do, and we have an understanding of the context in which they do it. The mission of the library media program in the school, which is to "ensure that students and staff are effective users of ideas and information," drives our field.

The rest of the education world is not out to get us, but at times we are ignored, which can be a far worse enemy. But school library media programs, because they are based on education best practices of reading encouragement, inquiry learning, and integration of technology, could be more central to the education world than they currently are. We practice what others preach.

Advocacy, defined as the creation of a supportive community, comes from engagement in the educational practices of the school and district, and modeling the best practices of each of those.

Research

There is little research to prove that advocacy creates stronger school library media programs, increases administrative or community support for such programs or their resources and or budgets, or has a positive impact on student achievement. We can't prove that advocacy works.

However, authors in the school library media field such as Gary Hartzell and Doug Johnson, in writing about the invisible and the indispensable librarian, make the commonsense point that strong advocacy in school library media programs makes the rest of such programs possible.[6]

Key Facts about Advocacy

If it is true that all politics is local, then it is also true that all advocacy is local as well. Although national programs have helped tremendously to focus efforts on school libraries at the national level, school library media specialists advocate for local programs, resources, services, and support every day.

The best way to use advocacy is to create an advocacy plan, based on the following.

Overarching goal. This type of goal is based on a pressing need for the school library media program. The need can be more resources and higher budgets, but these are actually the results of advocacy. Advocacy goals tend to be more focused on the way that other people feel about the library, such as increasing the visibility of the school library media program in the instructional process, or increasing the awareness of the impact of the school library media program on education.

Specific goals. These are goals for administrators, classroom teachers, parents, and even students. These goals are based on the overarching goal but are more specific. Suppose you want the administrator to think the library is more important than he or she does, or you may want parents to see the library as equal to the classroom in the learning process.

Activities. These are events, services, programs, or acts that you as a library media specialist will use to increase the chances that change will occur for the specific groups just listed. Newsletters, informative e-mails, and programs are all activities.

Assessments. How will you tell if your advocacy efforts are progressing? If you want to see more support from parents, then you could use head counts of the number of parents who stopped in during open house.

Advocacy has a direct relation to the NBPTS process in portfolio entry four, Documented Accomplishments, as well as making other entries easier. Advocacy is how we ensure that our work has meaning to others.

FLEXIBLE ACCESS

One of the most anxiety-ridden questions regarding National Board certification is: "Can I do this if I don't have flex access?" The answer is an unqualified yes. In fact, members of the Library Media Standards Writing Committee would say that the standards were written specifically so that all school library media specialists would have an equal chance of being nationally board certified.

Flexible access to the school library media center has long been considered a best practice. Even in the early days of the field, caution was raised about filling the school library media center with scheduled classes so much that it would prevent students, either individually or in classes, from using the facility or resources for a valid instructional purpose.

Background

Flexible access is defined by its opposite, a fixed schedule. In a fixed-schedule school library media center, classes of students are scheduled for the center on a regular basis for 30–45-minute blocks of time. During this class time, the classroom teacher is usually granted a planning period. Daily planning periods are an established custom for classroom teachers, and in unionized states they are mandated by contract as to their frequency and length. Even in non-unionized states, planning periods are the usual practice. Sometimes the school library media center used in this way is referred to as a "special." Other specials are art, music, physical education, and sometimes the computer lab.

For our purposes, a flex-scheduled school library media program is one in which the library media specialist is free to schedule classes, small groups, and individual students to maximize use of the library media center's resources and facilities. The schedule may, in the best interests of the students and for the routine of the classroom teacher, have a class coming into the library at the same time each week. However, the teacher is free to be present with the class, something that does not happen in a fixed-schedule situation.

Research

The most prominent researchers in the field of flexible access are Jean Donham and Donna Shannon.[7] In her 1996 research, Shannon documented the implementation and impact of flexible access in two Library Power elementary schools in Kentucky. Donham wrote about the use of flex access in collaborative skills instruction.

Research into instructional practices is usually criticized for its lack of a scientific basis. In true scientific research, one practice is compared to another under the same circumstances in order to see which practice is better. In education this is difficult, since it is hard to deliberately put children in circumstances in which a practice that is believed to be inferior to another is imposed upon the children, thereby denying them one that would be a better educational environment.

Although there has been much authoritative information in the research literature about flexible access, there has been little attempt to scientifically determine exactly what is better in school library media centers that have flex access. We know that flex access gives more opportunity for collaborative instruction. We also know that students may have more time to come to the library to check out books.

Sometimes it is not a question of fixed or flex schedules in the absolute. Some school library programs use a balance between fixed and flex. The upper elementary grades may be flexed, but the early grades may be fixed, so that their students have an opportunity to become acclimated to the library by checking out books and having a literature experience.

Those who question the use of flexible access point to the difficulties of ensuring that each child in the school has an equal opportunity to visit the library and check out books. Those using flex access must work with classroom teachers to ensure that students visit the library on a regular basis. Some classroom teachers are reluctant to be generous with time, and the library visit can be pushed off in favor of other classroom activities, or worse, used as either a reward or a punishment, instead of as a regular instructional activity that is just as important as math, social studies, or science.

Once a school has gotten used to being scheduled in this way, it is generally very difficult to change. Classroom teachers are undoubtedly hard-working, especially at the elementary level. They are in their classrooms before the start of the school day and welcome as many as thirty or more students each day. They settle them down for learning, and for the next six to seven hours are in charge, and sometimes sole charge, of their lives. Who would begrudge these teachers a mere thirty minutes to make parent phone calls, take a bathroom break, or prepare the instructional plans for the rest of the day?

The school library media specialist insisting on the change to flexible access will not find many friends in the teachers' lounge. It is difficult at best to convince a faculty to change, despite many articles in the literature regarding ways to encourage faculties and administrators to move toward this change.

Key Facts about Flexible Access

NBPTS candidates should be able to recognize flexible access as an accepted school library media best practice. They need to be able to define it, and discuss their school library media program within the context of that definition. If a candidate is in a situation where he or she has flex access, the benefits need to be discussed, as well as the continual need for advocacy with classroom teachers and administrators. If the school library media program is on a fixed schedule and provides the teachers with a planning period, the library media specialist needs to realize that these are not ideal conditions, and should probably mention that in the reflective essay accompanying the portfolio entries.

Most of the research and professional articles on flex access support the importance of advocacy in the implementation and maintenance of this best practice. School library media specialists must be proactive in ensuring that each faculty member and administrator understands the importance of an open schedule.

ACCESS

Flexible access used to be referred to as flexible scheduling, and since it is defined by the lack of a schedule, the term *flexible access* is probably more appropriate. However, *access* probably also crept into the title because of the focus today on access to libraries, in this case, the school library media center's programs, resources, and services.

Research

The most authoritative document on access for libraries is found in the *Library Bill of Rights*, adopted by the American Library Association in 1939 and periodically reaffirmed by that organization ever since.[8] The *Library Bill of Rights* has been kept up-to-date and appropriate through the development of various interpretations. One of these is the school library media interpretation, entitled "Access to Resources and Services in the School Library Media Program." This document outlines the tenets important to school library media centers. A few of these tenets are noted below.

The library is never closed. The school library media center must be open to students before, during, and after the school day. This means that the center is not closed and locked because there is a class using it, or because the school library media specialist is at lunch, or because the library is being used for a book fair. The school library is always open for one child to use. Of course, it is reasonable that there is a limited amount of seating, but like Jell-O, there is always room for one more use by one more student.

Students are not denied access because of age. Although it is reasonable to label sections of the library in order to help students find reading material more efficiently, students must be allowed the use of all materials in all formats.

Students are not denied access because of their ability to pay. The only way to ensure that one never has an overdue book is never to check one out. Some students learn this lesson very early, and avoid situations in which they will be forced to ask their parents for money that is not there.

Key Facts about Access

The library must be open and accessible to students throughout the entire school day, defined as before, during, and after school. This tenet is the first element in Martha Wilson's School Library Score Card, available in 1928 as an evaluation instrument for school libraries. It still holds true today.[9]

Students should not be denied access to library media programs, resources, and services because of age or grade level. Turned around, this also means that all resources in the school library should be available to students, such as videotapes, electronic resources, audiovisuals, and other resources as well. Books should not be denied to students because of behavioral or other problems.

It is usually illegal to suspend students from instructional activity without a superintendent's hearing. A student may be moved from one math class into another because of disruptive behavior, or may even be tutored if it is shown that no math teacher will tolerate that behavior. School library media specialists do not have the authority to decide that a student will be denied information resources or information skills. That authority lies with the principal or superintendent, and is reserved for only the most severe behavioral problems.

Hand in hand with access are intellectual freedom issues. The ALA's Office for Intellectual Freedom provides school library media specialists with a wealth of materials on this topic for review. With regard to intellectual freedom issues, school library media specialists should do the following.

Be aware of areas in which they self-censor the collection. Although many school library media specialists would swear this doesn't happen, discussions on cutting out advertisements from magazines because they are perceived to be inappropriate, or shredding the *Sports Illustrated* annual swimsuit issue, might cause some to think differently.

Be able to produce at a minute's notice the selection policy of the school district and the board-approved challenged materials policy. The school library media specialist should also have read these, be able to explain them, and be able to point parents to commonly used materials on the topic of intellectual freedom. Again, the materials from the Office for Intellectual Freedom are invaluable.

SUMMARY

The best practices discussed in this chapter outline just some of the areas outside the portfolio entries that are a part of excellence in school library media programming. It is important to recognize them.

Another way that these best practices can be addressed is in portfolio entry four, Documented Accomplishments. The school library media specialist's efforts to move toward the implementation of one of these best practices, such as increasing access to materials and resources, implementing flex access, or creating exciting advocacy programs in the school community, can be used very nicely in entry four. In order to improve library practice, school library media specialists must settle on a learning goal, then embark on professional development activities (reading professional journals, attending conference sessions) and share that information with colleagues.

The American Association of School Librarians (www.ala.org/aasl/) has many resources that are required reading for background information on best practices. The @ your library toolkit, the position statements, and the AASL Resource Guides should be read and should be used for reflective writing prompts. These materials are the basic building blocks of the profession.

Of course, as with all accomplishments that are worth documenting for the National Board, the accomplishments must be directed at having a positive effect on student learning. However, this is easy to prove with any of the best practices discussed in this chapter.

NOTES

1. The Knapp School Library Manpower Project in the 1950s and early 1960s created waves of change in the school library media field. As one part of the project, school librarians were surveyed to find the tasks they performed in school libraries. The result of that survey was the *Behavioral Requirements Analysis Checklist* (Chicago: American Library Association, 1973).
2. "Kids Who Read, Succeed" and "@ your library" are major advocacy initiatives of the American Library Association. More information can be found at http://www.ala.org.
3. See information regarding advocacy on the ALA website.
4. Gary Hartzell, "The Invisible School Librarian," *School Library Journal* 43 (November 1997): 24–29.
5. *Information Power* (Chicago: American Library Association) introduced national guidelines for school library media programs in 1986. A revised edition in 1998 further cemented *Information Power* as the guiding standards of the school library media field. Library Power, the Dewitt Wallace Reader's Digest grant program, greatly influenced the profession in its approach to school library media programs.

6. Gary Hartzell, *Building Influence for the School Librarian* (Worthington, OH: Linworth, 1994); and Doug Johnson, *The Indispensable Library: Surviving (and Thriving) in School Media Centers* (Worthington, OH: Linworth, 1997).
7. Donna Shannon, "Tracking the Transition to a Flexible Access Library Program in Two Library Power Elementary Schools," *School Library Media Quarterly* 24 (Spring 1996): 155–65; and Jean Donham van Deusen, "Prerequisites to Flexible Scheduling," in *Foundations for Effective School Media Programs*, ed. Ken Haycock (Englewood, CO: Libraries Unlimited, 1999).
8. The *Library Bill of Rights* and "Access to Resources and Services in the School Library Media Program" can be found on the website of the ALA's Office for Intellectual Freedom, at http://www.ala.org/ala/oif/statementspols/statementsif/librarybillrights.htm/.
9. Martha Wilson's School Library Score Card was originally published in the *School Library Yearbook* (Chicago: American Library Association, 1928). It is considered the first attempt to evaluate a school library program according to a standardized measure.

PART III *The Process*

In some ways, this book follows the outline of Robert Atkins's popular diet book. The first ten chapters of that book are filled with information about nutrition, how the body works, and why traditional diets and other weight-loss techniques are doomed to failure. The actual diet is not reviewed until the eleventh chapter. Atkins understood the nature of his readers, and at the beginning of chapter 11 he notes, "First, let me welcome those of you who are starting the book at this point," knowing that a *just tell me what to do* attitude will tempt many readers to skip over the background information needed for success.[1]

And so it is with the National Board for Professional Teaching Standards. The portfolio entries and assessment center exercises are overwhelming at first, as is opening the box with the labels of bar codes, pages of directions, and the discussion lists full of advice. It is tempting to page through this book, skipping over the background information on the

National Board process and the background information on school library media programs until this point, when the actual portfolio instructions are reviewed.

But consider first the problems that NBPTS had to solve in order to develop criteria and assessments for prospective National Board Certified Teachers. It had to develop some kind of test or assessment that would cover the broad range of standards, would be part of the normal professional practice in all grade levels, and would provide evidence of accomplished teacher status without being impossible to accomplish in a set period of time. For the school library media field, this means the portfolio entries and assessment center exercises have to be based on library media practice in all grade levels from kindergarten through grade 12. They have to be tasks, knowledge, and skills common to school library media specialists in large urban schools and small rural ones; with a large staff of several school library media specialists and several clerks and those with a sole professional and no support staff; for schools with a fixed schedule and those with flexible access; in schools that are models of technology, resources, and budgets and in schools that exist on frayed and tattered shoestrings.

In short, the NBPTS assessments have to meet what NBPTS calls the APPLE criteria:[2]

- Administratively feasible
- Professionally credible
- Publicly acceptable
- Legally defensible
- Economically affordable

This took time: in the case of the NBPTS library media assessment processes, almost two years, with a pilot year in which almost 900 school library media specialists piloted at least one of the assessments. An understanding of the relationship between the assessments and the standards process is crucial to performing well.

And so for those of you who started at the beginning of this book, it may have been tedious to wade through the school library media knowledge base on which the entries are based when you really want to get started on your portfolio. That time will benefit you now, however, as you read through each portfolio entry.

If you have started this book with this part, remember several points as you begin.

First, assessment is based on the standards. That means, as simple as it sounds, that the assessors will use the standards to grade the entries. The beginning of each portfolio entry notes which standards are covered. As you compile each of your portfolio entries, you will have to go back to the standards and reread them many times to make sure that you have encompassed the standards in your entry.

Second, the portfolio entries are based on accomplished teaching as defined in the field of school library media. The field is broad, with a rich history and defined best practices. In order to fully complete the entries, the successful candidate will need to know how the field got to where it is today.

Third, it's not enough to be good at performing isolated elements of a school library media program. Being good at what you do in the eyes of classroom teachers, parents, and school administrators is not a guarantee of success. The standards are divided into three areas: what accomplished school library media specialists know, what they do, and how they grow as professionals. The successful candidate must show that he or she is accomplished in all three of these areas, not just one.

Fourth, things change. This book may give information that may have changed by the time that you complete the process. A candidate may swear that NBPTS told him to handle a specific unique instance in his portfolio a certain way. Remember that the assessments are always evolving. NBPTS is the only definitive source for answers to questions about NBPTS assessments. Input is necessary, and gathering information from a variety of sources is a great idea, but NBPTS is the only valid source of information about the NBPTS process.

In the next few chapters, we will review each portfolio entry in detail, reaching back to previous chapters to fill in the details of each entry.

NOTES

1. Robert C. Atkins, *Dr. Atkins' New Diet Revolution* (New York: Quill, 2002), 121.
2. The APPLE criteria from NBPTS can be found at http://www.nbpts.org/standards/dev.clm.

9

Entry One: Instructional Collaboration

Clear, consistent, and convincing evidence of your ability to collaborate with a colleague to plan, develop, and implement an instructional sequence that links the library media program and its resources to a content area and to assess student work that results from the instructional collaboration.[1]

For recent graduates of library school, the collaborative teaching of information skills was probably a major part of at least one class. Even if the actual practice teaching did not include a collaborative lesson, understanding collaboration as a process was taught as a major component of the course. The names of Haycock, Loertscher, Turner, Stripling, Kuhlthau, and Eisenberg and Berkowitz are most likely as familiar to these graduates as are those of well-known authors of children's and young adult novels.[2]

For others, perhaps those more experienced in the field, collaboration with classroom teachers to integrate information skills into classroom content by partnering in the teaching process was not mentioned in library school. Perhaps, as in this author's preservice training decades ago, scheduled classes were encouraged, and preservice school library media specialists were told to shoo teachers out of the room so that students could see the library as a classroom; and so that parents, students, and classroom teachers would perceive the school library media specialist as the library teacher, in the same light as the social studies teacher, the music teacher, or the art teacher.

For those experienced in the field, collaboration may be something that is done, and perhaps done well, but an experienced library media specialist may not have the theory and background knowledge to discuss why collaboration is successful or unsuccessful.

It is always a misnomer to discuss the teaching act with only the teacher being involved. With any National Board portfolio entry, the focus must be on the students. The writer of this entry will find much in common with NBPTS candidates in other fields in the discussion of learning styles, in reflecting upon student progress, and in the descriptions of instruction. The manner in which the teaching and learning process is described by a science teacher, art teacher, or an elementary teacher is probably very similar to descriptions of student learning by the library media specialist.

The school library media entries, however, are one of the few NBPTS certification areas that require the active participation of another teacher in the teaching act. The collaborative teaching of information skills integrated into a subject area cannot be done alone. The classroom teacher must be deeply involved in the process, and consequently be deeply involved in the National Board entry process as well. In some cases, it may be wise to choose a classroom teacher who is working on his or her own National Board entry. This can evolve into a true collaborative partnership, since both partners are striving with equal effort to make the collaboration a success.

In most discussions of collaborative work with classroom teachers, the best advice for beginning the collaborative effort is usually to choose a teacher with whom you are comfortable and have collaborated with in the past. There are reasons for following that advice when approaching this entry. The classroom teacher will have to be involved in the entry development, and his or her teaching, while not directly critiqued, will certainly be noted. A teacher with a strong sense of self-esteem and confidence in his or her teaching skills is a good choice. Even more helpful are personality attributes such as flexibility, a high degree of trust, and the ability to adapt instruction to meet each other's instructional goals.

However, candidates should keep in mind that they will not be directly discussing the teacher much if at all in this entry, or in the other portfolio entries either. A good teaching partner is necessary to complete the entry, but the focus of the entry, as with all NBPTS work, is on the students. For that reason, it may be wise to choose a class with which you are familiar. If you know the students, are obviously at ease with them, and know their names, personalities, and especially their learning styles, you will have much more success in the entry. Add to that combination a partner teacher who values the integration of information skills into classroom content, and a successful partnership is more easily achieved.

WHAT WILL I NEED TO DO?

In this entry, you will need to teach a collaborative integrated information skills unit with one class. You will need to document the collaboration in some way, either through a planning log, a calendar, or other means. You will need to choose two students, and track their progress through the instructional unit.

You will not need to videotape the instruction. That is a part of entries two and three, but not of this entry.

The Tasks

Simply put, the Instructional Collaboration entry task is to teach a collaborative unit in conjunction with a classroom teacher. When reading the actual phrases used to introduce entry one in the portfolio instructions, the directions paint that task with a broader brush.

Accomplished library media specialists, in the key words and phrases taken from the portfolio entry, will demonstrate the following characteristics.

Rapport. The collaboration is not a one-time experience, but is based on a relationship with students, teachers, and members of the learning community. Collaboration is a culture, not an event.

Lead in the understanding of multiple literacies. Print, technology, information, visual, all of these literacies and more make up the school library media program. The school library media specialist functions as lead teacher in the schoolwide development of these literacies, and is recognized as such by the school community.

Partner with teachers to create, implement, and assess learning experiences. In other words, they co-plan, co-teach, and co-assess, yet the design of those experiences is not head down looking at the assignment and resources, but heads-up, looking at the goals of the school and district. The collaboration is deep as well as broad, and begins with curriculum development and the creation of school-level learning goals.

Continuous. Collaboration in a busy library media program cannot be isolated. The use of the library by the rest of the school cannot stop when one class is in the library. This entry specifically mentions collaboration in working with individuals, small groups, and large groups. Those actions are meant to be simultaneous.

Reflective. School library media specialists actively seek to better their practice by reflection and serious study. They base their analysis of instruction not on the smoothness of delivery or the presence of minimal distractions, but rather on student learning.

Read through the entry, and highlight those areas of particular importance to you. Strive to see the depth in the analysis. This is not just an isolated collaborative lesson, but rather a way to represent the depth of your program through a presentation of instructional collaboration. Preparing an NBPTS entry is like transforming sap from maple trees into maple syrup. It takes thirty-seven gallons of sap, boiled over long hours, to make one gallon of syrup. You need to read, study, and take notes and document the broad scope of your program, and then boil it down to the page limits set by NBPTS for its assessment procedures.

This entry is based on standards 1, 2, 3, 4, 6, and 7, as noted in figure 9-1.

It is important to review these standards carefully before beginning this entry, to refer again to the complete text of the standards during entry preparation, and again before declaring the entry complete. *Remember that the assessment is based on the standards, not the portfolio instructions.*

FIGURE 9-1 ■ *Standards Related to Entry One*

STANDARD 1	***Knowledge of Learners***
	Accomplished library media specialists have knowledge of learning styles and of human growth and development.
STANDARD 2	***Knowledge of Teaching and Learning***
	Accomplished library media specialists know the principles of teaching and learning that contribute to an active learning environment.
STANDARD 3	***Knowledge of Library and Information Studies***
	Accomplished library media specialists know the principles of library and information studies needed to create effective, integrated library media programs.
STANDARD 4	***Integrating Instruction***
	Accomplished library media specialists integrate information literacy through collaboration, planning, implementation, and assessment of learning.
STANDARD 6	***Administering the Library Media Program***
	Accomplished library media specialists plan, develop, implement, manage, and evaluate library media programs to ensure that students and staff use ideas and information effectively.
STANDARD 7	***Reflective Practice***
	Accomplished library media specialists engage in reflective practice to increase their effectiveness.

WHAT DO I SEND IN?

In preparing NBPTS portfolio entries, the videotape portion can sometimes overwhelm the preparation needed for the other parts of the entry. As noted earlier, this entry does not require a videotape of instruction. For that reason, this is a great entry to use for comparing how well you have answered the writing prompts, and comparing your writing against the standards. This entry requires the following:

Ten pages of written commentary. This commentary has specific
   parts and suggested page lengths.
Work samples from students. You will choose two students, and
   choose two samples of their work.
Evidence (documentation) to prove the collaborative aspect of the
   program
Cover sheets and forms

WHAT DO I HAVE TO WRITE?

The length limit for the entire written commentary is ten pages. Suggested page lengths are given for each section of the entry. These page lengths are suggestions, but it is wise to keep them in mind when beginning to prepare the entry. It may be a good idea at first to ignore the page length, and just get your thoughts down on paper. The use of a red pencil to slash and burn the bulk of late-night, bleary-eyed pages of writing may be painful, but it is better than attempting to keep the writing within the page limits at the beginning. Limiting your writing may cause you to miss an important piece of the entry.

You might also consider saving different versions of the entry. You may delete a section, then decide later that it was important. Saving entry1jan15, entry1feb2, and entry1mar10 as separate word-processed documents allows a change to be a matter of cutting and pasting rather than rewriting.

Focus on content, not size, until the entry has all of the content needed. Then the delete key can come into play, as the entry is whittled down to the requisite length. Sometimes it will seem that the writing prompts are repetitive, and the phrase "I just answered that!!" will come to mind. NBPTS will not ask the same question twice, so the information that you give will contain different yet crucial pieces of the story. The information must be consistent and must be focused on the instruction, yet it is not repetitive.

Not all of the written commentary is unique to each entry. For some of the sections, such as the Instructional Context at the very beginning, the writing prompts ask for much the same detail as entries two and three. The writing that you do for the Instructional Context for entry one will not be identical to that for entries two and three, but it can possibly be adapted for use in these other entries.

Qualitative researchers use the terms *dense* or *thick* to describe writing non-statistical qualitative research results.[3] This is the type of writing used in the National Board materials, in which every word and sentence in the standards and portfolio instructions adds meaning to the whole. This type of writing is crucial to the Instructional Context section, where a great deal of description must be packed into a one-page space.

The NBPTS portfolio instructions show examples of reflective writing. After writing to similar prompts, candidates should compare their writing to the NBPTS examples and make comments of *description* and *analysis and reflection* in the same way. Learning to identify these pieces is crucial.

Section One: Instructional Context (One Page)

Here you will describe your school, the class, the students, and your teaching context. You can also describe any other particular instructional challenges of the class or your teaching. This is an opportunity to talk about your fixed schedule, the difficulties of school culture, the students with special needs included in the class. Be careful that your writing does not whine or sound negative to the reviewer. Every classroom, every school, and every library program has unique qualities that are both opportunities and challenges. The lack of a flexible schedule, poor budgets, local economic issues, or school social issues are best reported as facts, neither painting a too-bright picture nor whining about the impossibilities of change. This should be an opportunity to explain your program in the context of the school.

It is not necessary to have the perfect instructional context or the ideal library media center facility, collection, budget, or schedule. Sometimes, in fact, the lack of perfection provides an opportunity to showcase your instructional adaptability and flexibility where a perfect situation would not. Classroom management, for example, is much more difficult when there are many students in the library media center. Yet this may explain why you chose the instructional methodology or research skills strategies that you used. A busy library media center program can never be a negative.

What is important is whether you can demonstrate that you know what the best practices of the school library media profession dictate. Whether or not you have that particular ideal as your reality is secondary. Being able to demonstrate accomplished teaching skills in a less-than-perfect situation is far preferable to presenting a sterile facility in which nothing exciting ever happens.

Section Two: Planning for Instruction (Two Pages)

In the scoring rubric, you will find a list of questions to be answered regarding the planning of instruction. Make sure that you have answered each of these questions. They center on the planning process, including the setting of instructional goals and the choices for delivery of instruction. You will also have to explain your role and responsibilities in all parts of the instructional process. Good documentation and careful journaling after each planning session will help you articulate the decisions made regarding your role.

Many times candidates ask to see examples of collaborative planning logs. The manner in which the information is kept, such as a spreadsheet, word document, handwritten journal, or even on daily calendars is not as important as the information that is recorded. Although a scribbled note with a few phrases may work to trigger reminders for busy library media specialists, assessors cannot read your mind, nor can they assume what your key phrases mean. The entry one planning log will have to be more in-depth than the one used in day-to-day work.

You will have to discuss your teaching style. Is it constructivist or direct instruction? What research methodologies did you choose? Were they I-search or Big6, or another methodology? Remember that regardless of how well you can discuss any of these, the reasons for choosing one must be able to be tied back to the students. Although all teachers feel more comfortable with a particular methodology than others, and all teaching repertoires are unique to individual teachers, the purpose of teaching always returns to whether or not the students learned.

Section Three: Analysis of Instruction and Student Work (Five Pages)

Again, the scoring rubric gives a list of questions to be answered regarding the students. This set of questions focuses on the implementation of instruction, and how you integrated resources and library media services into that instruction.

To answer these questions, it may be necessary to review the issues surrounding your selection of materials and the collection development process. Although many school library media practitioner journals offer lists of resources matched with subject areas or specific curriculum topics, it is rare for them to give the reasons why specific resources might be helpful to use with particular students. Even more rare is how the use of these resources helped students learn. This conversation goes beyond matching the reading level of the resource to the reading level of the student; it examines how the resource can be transformed from an interesting read to one that is integral to the instructional process.

All teachers, including school library media specialists, frequently describe the instructional process but rarely analyze or reflect on it. Practice is needed to move from a description of context, instructional plan, resources used, and the degree to which students learned to a true analysis of and reflection on the instructional process.

Section Four: Reflection (Two Pages)

The directions for this section suggest that the candidate refer to the collaboration plan and the student work samples. At first glance, it may be difficult to conceive of filling up two pages with reflection. However, remember that accomplished teachers are reflective practitioners. They think deeply about their instruction on a daily basis. It may be wise to spend time thinking about this section.

Specific prompts for reflection include whether or not the instructional goals were met and what you would change about the lesson to improve it, given the same situation again. You might also want to project the importance of this unit in the learning processes that students will face at a later time, either later this year or in their educational future.

DOCUMENTATION OF COLLABORATION

I once knew an eighth-grade history teacher who would throw an essay test in the general direction of his students and say, "who, what, where, when, why important?" Those directions seem to be applicable to this section on the documentation of collaboration. Assessors need to understand the depth of collaboration as it unfolded, and the essay based on "who, what, where, when, why important?" may encompass what the assessors will want to know.

Candidates will need to take detailed notes for each planning session they have. Although there is no predetermined magic number for the number of times that instructional partners should meet in order to have a successful collaborative experience, at least one time should probably be a face-to-face meeting, not a pass-by in the hall. Document everything, including e-mail exchanges, talks over lunch, and after-school drop-ins.

It could be that a fixed schedule precludes you from planning with teachers as a group, or even with individual teachers during their planning periods. If that is true, then documentation of how you plan collaborative experiences with colleagues is extremely important.

WHICH STUDENTS TO CHOOSE?

Choose interesting students. The portfolio instructions suggest that you select students who will give you a chance to discuss your practice. It may be helpful to choose two very different students. The best-performing students are not always a good choice for this. Remember that the assessors will be looking not for the degree to which the students learned, but rather for your ability to analyze their learning progress.

Students who may have learning challenges will give you so much more to write about than perfect students who turn in perfect student work and exhibit perfect student behavior. Students who are challenges, who need your intervention for them to learn, will give you an opportunity to show your involvement in the learning process. You might also be able to add information about your work with students who have documented special needs, and your progress in accommodating those needs.

Two students who are matched exactly in their learning progress will also not provide as much rich detail about teaching and learning strategies as will those who are progressing at different rates. It is unusual that two students who have started at two different places in their learning progress (as any two students would do) have ended up at the exact same spot.

SELF-ASSESSING YOUR WORK

Remember that in all of the portfolio entries you must show clear, convincing, and consistent evidence that you have met the requirements; in other words, that you have the knowledge and skills and have engaged in the reflective practice of the accomplished teacher. The evidence is based on the standards, not the portfolio entries.

To achieve a 4-point score on this entry, which is the highest possible score, you should have provided clear, consistent, and convincing evidence of the following, according to the portfolio instructions.

Did the evidence show that your collaboration extended from the very beginning of the project to the very end? In other words, from the early co-planning stage to the ending co-assessment of student progress?

Was the unit high-quality and with high expectations for student performance? Was it student-centered? Lessons on the Dewey decimal system or dictionary skills are sometimes rote ones with little meaning for the classroom teacher, school library media specialist, or the students. What does it mean that you taught a lesson today? How important was it for the students to learn it, and did they engage in the learning process?

Did you demonstrate that you had an understanding of student learning styles and that you incorporated that knowledge into your teaching? When you discussed the work of the two students, was this apparent?

Did you show your knowledge of the library and information science field, that you have a broad ability to select and use resources in instruction, and that you incorporate technologies effectively?

Were you a full partner in the assessment of student work? This does not mean that you had the responsibility of reading papers on advanced placement biology topics. It does mean, however, that the skills that you taught were as important to the classroom teacher and to the students as the biology skills, that you were not an add-on or a good-conduct grade.

Did your reflection illustrate the broad sense of the entire library program? Remember that this entry is not designed to show collaboration in a single lesson, but rather uses the context of a single lesson to showcase the collaborative instructional program in the school library media center.

Did you describe the collaboration, instruction, and learning process? Did you analyze the effectiveness of the instruction? Did you reflect on the collaborative process in the context of the school library media program?

It may help to read back through your entry after it is written, looking for the answers to each of the questions posed above. It also may help to use an interview concept, with a learning partner (child or adult) asking those questions as if you are on a job interview. This will give you a fresh perspective on whether or not you fully answered the questions.

Grade your entry (or ask someone else to grade it) using the levels. Understand why your entry is only a 2, or even a 1. Constantly reflecting on the assessor's viewpoint will strengthen your perspective.

SUMMARY

In the narrowest sense, this entry is merely a collaborative unit, but in a broader sense it is illustrative of the entire library media program. This entry will be easiest for those who regularly collaborate with classroom teachers to integrate information skills into classroom content, who strive to encourage more teachers to collaborate, and who actively seek to increase student learning of information skills. In other words, this entry will be easiest for those school library media specialists who are accomplished teachers of information skills.

The lack of a videotaped element for this entry can be perceived as both positive and negative. Certainly it takes less time to prepare the entry without watching and rewatching the videotape. On the other hand, it can make the writing for this entry more difficult, since the written description of the library program becomes crucial. Assessors will know only what they read about the library, the school, and the students. They will not be able to see the program except through the words that candidates write.

Candidates who think, write, and talk about their program to others in the school and library community often will have an advantage over those candidates who do not.

When looking back over this entry, make sure that you have told a consistent story. If you discuss elaborate collaborative planning meetings, but in the instructional context you mentioned that you have a fixed schedule with virtually no time to plan, the assessors will wonder which story to believe. Check your facts to make sure that you have given a thorough but accurate picture of the library.

In the next few chapters, which discuss entries two and three, it will become evident that they too require some degree of collaboration. In some sense, all of the first three portfolio entries are collaborative in nature, and candidates may be able to literally have three different applications for one instructional sequence. Choosing which of the instructional sequences will be used for this particular entry may be difficult, however. Read the instructions, the writing prompts, and the standards to help decide.

It may be wise to work on entries two and three first and then come back to this entry at a later time, when those are finished. "Videotape early and videotape often" remains sage advice. If all classes that are potential entries for this and the other two instructional entries are videotaped, then candidates can use whichever class is most appropriate for each of the entries. If several classes are not videotaped because entry one does not require it, it will not be possible to decide at a later time to use one of those classes for another entry.

Food for Thought

When you are almost finished writing, print a rough draft and then color code the writing prompts with different colored pencils or highlighters. Go back through the document and highlight where you have answered each prompt. This will show you quickly where you have given a question only a brief surface answer, and not the deep reflection required for NBPTS success.

Do this same exercise with the standards. Have you referred back to the standards fully? There may be some standards that require more text than others, but each of the standards on which this entry is based should have been addressed.

School librarians spend part of their time pulling resources from the shelves to use with student research or enrichment topics. Think about each resource that you are pulling from the shelves. Why did you select that particular resource? Which students in the class will find it particularly useful? What will students gain by using this resource over another one? Write a reflective essay that is one-third description of the resource, one-third analysis on how it was used, and one-third reflection on what it means to the instructional process that the resource was used by a specific student.

NOTES

1. National Board for Professional Teaching Standards, *Early Childhood through Young Adulthood: Library Media: Scoring Guide* (Arlington, VA: National Board for Professional Teaching Standards, 2004), 19.
2. For a list of works by these authors, see the "Further Reading" section in chapter 3.
3. Yvonna S. Lincoln and Egon G. Guba, *Naturalistic Inquiry* (Beverly Hills, CA: Sage, 1985).

10 Entry Two: Literature Appreciation

Clear, consistent, and convincing evidence of the library media specialist's ability to foster an appreciation of literature in students by helping them to make inferences and interpretations of literature, to establish a library media center setting that is inviting and supportive, and to provide equal access for all students.[1]

Of all the National Board entries, Entry Two: Literature Appreciation seems to create the most consternation among school library media candidates. School library media specialists will often say that the reason they entered the field is to bring children and literature closer together. Encouraging the love of reading remains one of the dearest philosophical and emotional tenets of the field. So why shouldn't this entry be a "piece of cake" for school library media NBPTS candidates?

The first and most important point in the clarification of this entry is to read the definition of *literature*. The National Board says the following: "For the purposes of this entry, the terms literature and literary materials include any form of written work, including, but not limited to print fiction or nonfiction, print or electronic reference materials, textual information online, poetry, criticism, etc."[2] This entry moves from a simple sharing of a story with children or designing a book display to a range of possibilities that could include electronic sources or reference materials.

Although the entry allows for a wide range of materials that could be considered works of literature, candidates will have to consider their strengths in deciding what types of works of literature could be included. A knowledge of the more traditional definitions of children's and young adult literature cannot be avoided entirely in the NBPTS process, however. One of the assessment center exercises, discussed in chapter 13, is based on literature and requires a thorough knowledge of a wide range of print resources. For this portfolio entry, candidates may likewise want to think broadly about the range of literature choices as defined.

Certainly, using a work of children's or young adult fiction is not prohibited; in fact, most candidates probably still base entry two on traditional children's or young adult print literature. Candidates must remember that they are not necessarily limited to the fiction section when choosing literature, however. Indeed, candidates often report success using nonfiction, poetry, or other print works as well.

Many NBPTS candidates feel that literature knowledge and appreciation is their strongest area within their professional field, and some are unpleasantly surprised when they receive their score on this entry. At times candidates have discussed a grade level bias with this entry, feeling that the entry is easier for elementary school library media specialists than for middle or high school ones.

One possible reason for both unexpectedly low scores and a perceived difficulty for high school librarians lies in the requirements of the entry, which goes far beyond a simple encouragement of reading or story-sharing. There are four specific points in the entry. The first, fostering an appreciation of literature, is traditional and part of most, and hopefully all, school library media programs. The library collection must connect to the users, their diverse interests, needs, and abilities. The second piece focuses on creating an environment in the library media center that encourages literature appreciation. This can be achieved through book displays, promotions, comfortable seating, and by creating policies that seek to remove barriers to open access. Both of these points are emphasized heavily in the literature of the field as well as in graduate school curricula.

Third, candidates must show that the literature activities in the library are integrated with what is being taught in the classroom. Perhaps this is not achieved perfectly in every literature appreciation activity in a school library media program, but most library media specialists would say that they make an attempt to integrate the literature activities in the library with what is happening in the classroom. They may admit to not making the connection as explicit as this entry directs, but they will testify to the need to make literature activities in the school library media center connect with the classroom. The stories selected for book-talking or story reading should have themes, plots, or characters that are related to the current classroom content.

It is the fourth element, "provide evidence of how you guide students to make inferences or interpretations about the literature used in the lesson," that creates a lull in the conversation when this entry is discussed. This point means the entry is about more than just presenting a structure to encourage reading, or presenting works to children in the hope of encouraging them to read. This entry, very specifically, requires interaction either among the students or between the teacher and students that is focused on the work of literature. Some school library media specialists, especially at the high school level, frankly admit that this is not the type of activity that frequently, or even ever, happens in their school library media center.

For the rationale behind the requirements for this entry, it is necessary to refer back to the essence of the core propositions of NBPTS. This is a teaching certification. Simply exposing children to literature in the hope that they will become readers by a strange combination of osmosis and atmospheric pressure is not teaching. We cannot just organize the structure of the library and indirectly hope that students take advantage of that structure. Our acceptance of the teaching role is what makes the school library different from other types of libraries. To be nationally board certified as a teacher, then, it is rational and logical that every aspect of our job must be seen by the NBPTS assessors through a teaching lens.

Far from changing what school library media specialists do, this entry provides new opportunities for collaboration with classroom teachers in the area of literature appreciation.

WHAT WILL I NEED TO DO?

The key points in the description of this activity are the following.

All students, regardless of developmental levels, must engage in the full range of activities. In what ways does your library collection encompass the learning abilities and exceptionalities of the entire student body? We need to celebrate the differences in our library's collection when compared between schools. The term *core collection* loses some of its meaning when all of its resources are narrowly aligned with the range of learning in the school.

Adjust. This is a key word in the second paragraph. It is assumed that the school library media specialist is flexible with the space, groupings of students, and the use of equipment. One way to ensure access is to continue to encourage students to use the widest array of materials possible.

Passion for reading. School library media specialists are passionate and open about the encouragement of reading. They are passionate because they believe in the power of reading to positively affect all aspects of a student's life. They are open because they know that the definition of reading is not limited to a certain type of material, on a narrow reading level, and with a certain level of literary merit.

Analysis for improvement. School library media specialists actively seek to improve reading through risk-taking behavior and trial and error. They will allow a child to check out a book far above or below that child's reading level simply because he or she wants to, and they know that the habit of checking out books must be carefully nurtured. They will figure out ways for pre-readers to conduct research because literature appreciation habits should begin early.

The Literature Appreciation entry is based on standards 1, 2, 3, 6, 7, and 9, as noted in figure 10-1. *Remember, the assessment is based on the standards, not on the portfolio entry instructions.*

FIGURE 10-1 ■ *Standards Related to Entry Two*

STANDARD 1	***Knowledge of Learners***
	Accomplished library media specialists have knowledge of learning styles and of human growth and development.
STANDARD 2	***Knowledge of Teaching and Learning***
	Accomplished library media specialists know the principles of teaching and learning that contribute to an active learning environment.
STANDARD 3	***Knowledge of Library and Information Studies***
	Accomplished library media specialists know the principles of library and information studies needed to create effective, integrated library media programs.
STANDARD 6	***Administering the Library Media Program***
	Accomplished library media specialists plan, develop, implement, manage, and evaluate library media programs to ensure that students and staff use ideas and information effectively.
STANDARD 7	***Reflective Practice***
	Accomplished library media specialists engage in reflective practice to increase their effectiveness.
STANDARD 9	***Ethics, Equity, and Diversity***
	Accomplished library media specialists uphold professional ethics and promote equity and diversity.

WHAT DO I SEND IN?

This entry requires both a videotape and written materials. The videotape will have two distinct parts. One part is a two-minute narrated pan of your library.

The second part is a fifteen-minute segment of a lesson. Each of these parts of the videotape must be uninterrupted. In other words, you will tape the two-minute pan, and at a later time, tape the fifteen-minute segment. You cannot stop the tape during either of these segments.

This entry requires a maximum of twelve pages of commentary written according to specific prompts. In this commentary you will talk about your library as well as your instructional lesson. You will also send up to four pages of instructional materials that you have used in the lesson shown on the videotape.

MAKING THE VIDEOTAPE

Ahh, the dreaded videotape. In one of my school library media preparation classes, I ask each of my students to make a two-minute narrated videotape of the school library media facility. This tape is not graded, but I assign it for several reasons. First, I use it to get a sense of the library that is being virtually renovated for the assignment. Second, I assign it as a practice skill for attempting NBPTS certification. And third, videotaping is a good exercise in visual perception. Some students have said that they never really saw their school library until they looked at it through the lens of a video camera.

Each semester I ask the students how long it took them to make the two-minute tape. For most of the students it took about four hours, sometimes in multiple sessions. This is a non-graded videotape that only I will see, and only in conjunction with one assignment for one library science class.

Even experienced home videographers have a sense of finality when picking up a video camera for an assignment. They feel pressured to make sure that it is perfect, yet the inevitability of a flaw, a stutter or mumble, or of a part of the library shown too fast or too slow creates a tension that is only partially resolved by a retake. And of course, the retake once again presents the chance for other flaws to mar the videotape's perfection.

With this time commitment in mind for a videotape in which quality has no negative connotations, is not graded, and is a minor part of an assignment, how long will it take a candidate to make a two-minute narrated pan of the library for an NBPTS entry? Most of the time, the answer is several days. Note that it shouldn't have to take that long, but most candidates would probably agree that it most likely will.

As stated previously, there are two types of video that you must put on one tape for this entry. One is a two-minute narrated pan, and the other is a fifteen-minute unedited segment from a single lesson.

For the two-minute pan, most candidates have tried to find a time when the library was not occupied or otherwise used. If you feel that having students, teachers, or administrators in the library would be helpful to your written reflection about the use of the library, by all means include them, but remember that you must have a signed permission form on file for every person being shown, regardless of age. If you choose to videotape an empty library, most candidates find that after school or on Saturday mornings may be a good time.

The method for obtaining a pan varies. One of the most unusual is the rotating husband method. One candidate reported that her husband sat on a kitchen barstool, with the video camera balanced on his shoulder. As she narrated the videotape she slowly rotated the barstool, ensuring a smooth pan. Most candidates find it easiest to have someone else run the camera while they do the talking. Other candidates write a two-minute script, so that they can memorize the script with their eyes on a clock or stopwatch and have the timing perfect.

The tension of multitasking the narration and the videotaping can be minimized. Try taping the narration on a good-quality audiotape, then playing it back as you rotate the camera. This will ease the tension, yet ensure that you are staying under the two-minute limit.

Libraries come in all shapes and sizes. One large room is perfect to slowly pan across, but that may not be your library. If you have warrens, L-shapes, two libraries connected by an office, or a two-floor library, you may want to ask NBPTS what your options are in the videotape. This is also a great question to throw out on the discussion list. All libraries are unique, but the chances are that someone has a library just like yours.

Regardless of the method, remember that once the basic logistical requirements for the video are met, then content takes over. The quality of the video itself will not be assessed, nor the skills of the videographer. The videotaping qualifications only enable the video to be at an assessable level. Once that level is met, it is the content that scores the points. A flaw in the taping, if the content is perfect, is always better than the reverse.

When writing about the two-minute tape, candidates should be able to use the video to describe the choices that have been made in the development of the collection, along with the organization of both the collection and the room itself. A great middle-school library media specialist once had the idea of organizing the fiction section by genre. She had separate sections, both visually and in the library catalog, for horse books, mysteries, animals, romances, action-adventure, and other genres popular with middle-school students. Although this made shelving and cataloging more difficult, she was able to show data on the improved circulation as a direct result of this change. If she chooses to apply for National Board certification, she can use that data, justified with her reasons based on the reading interests of middle-school students found in her professional reading, to indicate that having a section of books that middle schoolers could find on their own was important.

The students in that school did not have to rely on the catalog's inadequate subject descriptions for fiction books, but instead relied on the library media specialist's desire to give middle schoolers enamored with books a special section filled with their specific reading interests. The library was organized for their needs; they did not have to modify their needs to fit the organizational requirements of the school library media center.

Not many candidates have taken such drastic measures to organize their collection, but you may have made decisions that in other ways made the library more accessible. Keep reading the standards, and find the elements that you can show about your program just from watching the videotape. The assessor will have no way of knowing why these elements exist or the story behind them unless you write about them.

For the fifteen-minute segment, you should be teaching a lesson that demonstrates how you meet the elements of this entry. Remember that the entry stresses both understanding and appreciation. You may be the most wonderful storyteller in the world, but a fifteen-minute segment showing you telling the story, even if you can show the entrancement of the students, does little to help with their understanding, and does nothing to assess the depth of understanding that the students gained.

WHAT DO I HAVE TO WRITE?

As part of this entry, you will need twelve pages of written commentary along the following guidelines.

Section One: Instructional Context (Two Pages)

This section of the entry is very much like the Instructional Context section required for entry one. There are perhaps more details required, but the other aspects are the same. Of course, the classes that you will be using for this assessment will be different, but the context is the same. To prepare for writing about this context, a school library media candidate may want to practice using classes that have been in the library frequently. What do you really know about the students that are seen? Can you discuss how the characteristics of the class influenced your instructional strategies? Do you know which students have special needs, and what accommodations you have made to address those needs?

At times the writing prompts will direct you to cite from the videotape. It may be tempting to interpret that as referring briefly, giving parallel information, or other indirect means. This is probably a mistake. Think of a direction to cite information from a print source. If you were directed to do that, you would find specific information, copy it down word for word, and then cite it directly using proper citation style and page number. Now translate this into citing from a videotape. You won't use citation style, but the other imperatives are the same. The assessor knows only the information that you choose to give. Following the directions exactly as written is extremely important.

Section Two: Organizing the Library Media Center (Two Pages)

This section is based on the two-minute pan of the library media center. The reflection asks two basic questions. First, how does the library collection meet the goals of this lesson and the needs, interests, and abilities of the students? Next, how do you promote areas of your collection to foster an appreciation of literature?

Remember as you write this entry that the definition of *literature* is important. The library media center collection may extend beyond the walls of the center and may consist of more than just those works that are shelvable. Community resources, Internet resources, government documents, and pamphlets, as well as fiction books for parallel reading and traditional nonfiction and reference works, are all part of the library media collection. Taking the particular lesson in mind, how well does the collection meet the lesson goals?

Remember also that your response in this section is based on the description and analysis of the videotape pan. It may be easy to wander off track when dealing with this broad question. Remain focused on the directions and the narrow focus of the question. After finishing a rough draft, you may want to highlight responses that are directly based on the videotape. This will help you to see the focus of your responses.

Section Three: Planning and Analysis of Instruction (Six Pages)

The directions for this section ask the candidate to focus on the fifteen-minute instructional segment. The questions are very specific in nature. Although six pages may seem daunting at first, they will fill up fast. There are eight very specific questions to answer regarding the instruction shown on the videotape.

Before beginning to write this section, reflect for several minutes on its title, Planning and Analysis of Instruction. The title reflects the heart of this entry. It is not nearly so much about what you did (the assessors can see that on the tape) but why you decided to do what they are seeing. Much instruction in schools, and indeed in school libraries, takes place without conscious thought. A class comes in, we introduce resources, they use the resources with our help, and the class leaves. At no time during that process are questions being answered such as those being asked in this entry, questions such as the following ones.

What do you know about these students who are about to enter the library? Do you know their learning abilities, exceptionalities, their motivation to learn?

Assuming that you know the above, what instructional methodologies will work best with this class matched with this assignment? Which one should be used? Constructivism? Direct instruction? Mastery learning?

What do you want these students to learn? Apart from using the resources, is there a larger instructional goal? Why is that goal important?

Not all of the questions in this section are as hard as these. This section also asks for information on the resources selected, and the reasons why they were selected. Most school library media specialists will find easy answers to questions about why the resources were selected, what other resources could be chosen, and how those resources met the subject area.

By far the hardest question to answer, and according to the discussion lists, the one that causes the most angst, is the following: "What instructional strategies did you use to guide students to make inferences or interpretations about literature through teacher-to-student and/or student-to-student interactions? What were your reasons for using these procedures and strategies? Cite specific examples from the videotape."

Rarely do we take students through the processes asked about here. In fact, in some NBPTS meetings, school librarians are genuinely confused over this. Questions such as "So are we acting as the English teacher?" reflect this confusion. In other discussions, there is anger at this part of the entry being supposedly easier for elementary school library media specialists than for secondary school ones.

What has not been discussed to much extent is the definition of "inferences or interpretations." This could be as simple as comparing and contrasting two different works, such as a book made into a movie, or interpretations of different websites, or even using spoofs of literature. Remember that even though the emphasis is on inferences and interpretations, it is also on the interactive aspect. The video must clearly show the students interacting with each other or with the teacher regarding the literature. When writing for this section, specific examples from the videotape must be shown.

Section Four: Reflection (Two Pages)

This section lists the specific areas for reflection. In the recommended two pages, candidates are directed to reflect on the student learning in this entry. In order to do well on this section, it is imperative that the candidate has thoughtfully answered each of the questions in the previous section. It will be impossible to answer whether or not the goals were successfully completed if the candidate has not clearly defined what those goals were.

Goals to simply "use resources" will only lead to the question of whether or not the resources were used. However, if students were intended to make a wise selection of resources instead, then the assessment piece can be a reflection on student learning. The entry also mentions the word *evidence*. Think of this entry as a courtroom. How do you know that the entry was successful? How can you tell?

INSTRUCTIONAL MATERIALS

The instructional materials to be submitted for this entry are not intended to be direct instruction worksheets. Instead, anything that can help illustrate the lesson can be included. This may include screenshots from websites, transparencies, sketches of notes or drawings put on a chalk- or whiteboard at the front of the class, or even descriptions of the materials used.

This is an opportunity for the candidate to show the assessors the materials that are being used in the videotape. The assessors can then follow the lesson that you are teaching. This is an important point for this entry. Do not assume that because you are not handing anything out to the students that you are not using instructional materials. In fact, ask yourself if there can be a lesson with no instructional materials. Unless you are standing in front of the class lecturing without notes, there has to be something that is considered an instructional material.

By the same token, do not swamp the assessor with extraneous material. Remember that the instructional materials you send should relate directly to what the assessor is watching. Confusion is not a good thing for an assessor to feel when turning extraneous pages of instructional materials. You are limited to sending four pages of instructional materials. Plan the instruction carefully to ensure that the materials reflect the work that you have put into this lesson.

Note also the directions for the format of the instructional materials. It would be foolish to have the instructional materials left unviewed because they did not conform to the specific sizes and fonts that the assessors required.

SUMMARY

When approaching this portfolio entry, it is crucial to remember that it must be completed from a teaching perspective. Public libraries usually have children's, young adult, and even adult programs based on literature. While these can be quite good, they are not intended to have an instructional goal. They are programs, not instruction. Some school library media specialists move out of the teaching mode and into the program mode when conducting a literature appreciation exercise. Candidates must remember that they are scored as teachers in all aspects of the application process.

In fact, candidates may find that the lesson chosen for this activity could just as easily have been chosen for Entry One: Instructional Collaboration. As an example, a school library media specialist decided to introduce graphic novels as part of a collaborative project with a ninth-grade U.S. history project. She used a historical fiction graphic novel, then discussed with students the elements of a graphic novel as compared with the elements of more traditional historical fiction. As a collaborative assessment, the students then researched a topic in U.S. history and created a storyboard for a graphic novel.

Lessons have plans, are based on instructional goals, are delivered according to some instructional methodology based on learner needs, and are assessed to ascertain learner progress in meeting those instructional goals. This is a literature appreciation lesson, not just a literature appreciation activity.

This entry also gives the candidate a chance to show the many ways that reading and literature are encouraged in the library media facility, through displays, posters, and through the narration on the videotape (e.g., "this is where the book club meets on Wednesday after school"). It also requires a knowledge of resources and of the curriculum of the school, and how those two integrate.

Because it is based on literature, entry two is sometimes perceived as the entry for which candidates believe they will receive their highest score. It can still be the strongest entry, but this will take a teaching mind-set throughout the entry, rather than a simple storytelling show-and-tell approach.

Food for Thought

What does the videotape show? Take a fresh copy of the standards and highlight elements that you see when watching the videotape, both the narrated pan and the fifteen-minute lesson segment. It is surprising what the video lens can show.

Once you are organized for the National Board process, you may be tempted to begin writing. The Instructional Context section of each entry is a good place to start. Its details are much the same for entries one, two, and three, so you can begin describing your school, community, and specific classes. Jot down notes on the instructional context of a particular class once a week or so. You may discover threads about the school community that you previously missed.

NOTE

1. National Board for Professional Teaching Standards, *Early Childhood through Young Adulthood: Library Media: Scoring Guide* (Arlington, VA: National Board for Professional Teaching Standards, 2004), 25.
2. Ibid., 143.

11

Entry Three: Integration of Technology

The most striking element in reading the specific direction for this entry is the use of the word *technologies*. From the entry's title, one would think that this is a lesson on technology skills, such as how to use PowerPoint, how to use a digital camera, or some other "how to." The standards, portfolio instructions, and scoring guide, however, steer the careful reader into two distinct areas. The first is the use of technologies to connect with instructional goals, and the second is the importance of information ethics. In other words, the emphasis of the entry is on the use of technology to support instruction, not instruction to support the use of technology. This is an extremely important distinction for candidates to make.

This entry, as well as the previous two, is based on the integration of the library media program into the life of the school. The lesson that you choose for this entry is probably one that could well have been used for the Instructional Collaboration entry, since a collaboration piece would certainly strengthen this entry. It might also be difficult to choose between a lesson that could have been used for the literature entry and one for this entry, since the broad definition of *literature* could well include literature based on information technology.

Clear, consistent, and convincing evidence of the library media specialist's ability to demonstrate effective and appropriate selection and integration of technologies into an instructional lesson to enhance student learning and to foster student understanding of the ethical and legal use of information.[1]

132

In any case, candidates must keep in mind that this entry is not just about teaching students to use technology. The technology must be used in an instructional context. In other words, teaching students to use PowerPoint is not acceptable, unless the use of PowerPoint is required for an instructional purpose.

Some years ago, in discussions with an instructional technologist, I asked what the instructional use of a digital camera was. His answer was that students needed to learn how to use it, and my retort was that the need to learn the function of a piece of equipment, if that was the only reason, was not good enough to require instructional time. For the next several months, whenever we met, he brought up the issue again, and noted that he was still thinking about it. Adding glitzy gadgetry to instruction has to go beyond just providing students with a motivation to become experts in technological bells and whistles. We cannot simply add technology because we feel that teaching students to click on the right buttons in the right order is a lifelong learning skill.

There has to be an added value to the inclusion of technology in learning. There are probably many instructional reasons for teaching students to use digital cameras. However, unless a candidate can articulate what those reasons are, then it is best not to use that lesson for this entry. When audiovisual materials were first used in teaching, it was stressed that they should be used only when the instructional process would be poorer without them, when they could show something that could not otherwise be seen, such as a time-lapse motion picture of a flower opening, or the geography of a foreign country. This was a hard lesson to learn then for audiovisual lovers, and it is a harder lesson still for technophiles now.

The key question to ask is, "What is the instructional purpose of this activity?" If the answer centers on the technology, then that lesson is most likely not a good fit for this entry.

In this entry candidates are asked to integrate technology into instruction. In a larger sense, they are integrating that technology not just into the library, not just into the classroom, but into the school community. They will do this by showing the following.

Integrate technologies into a single lesson.

Increase student understanding of the ethical or legal use of information.

Demonstrate your knowledge of content area curricula, and draw connections between student content area knowledge and the effective use of technology.

Show knowledge of library and information studies.

Reflect on your ability to do the above.

WHAT WILL I NEED TO DO?

The importance of effective teaching, as with the other entries, is the foundation of entry three as well. Contained in this foundational base is the need to account for students' differing interests, needs, and abilities in the design of instructional strategies. In this entry, candidates should be able to draw a close connection between individual student characteristics and instructional planning and delivery.

Candidates will need to remember that this entry is designed to show an area of strength for accomplished teachers in the teaching field of library media. All teaching fields have the responsibility to integrate technology as a teaching tool, but school library media has an especially strong link to technology both as a teaching tool and as an informational tool. Although many school library media specialists have strong technology skills, and in fact may serve as the network specialist or webmaster for their school, this is not the time to show off a knowledge of technology skills isolated from the teaching act.

In the same way, it is best to choose a technology with which you have a fairly high comfort level. The degree of technological skills of the assessors is not known. But using technology incorrectly will show your lack of knowledge and skill, especially if the assessor knows the technology well. Choose something you know already to illustrate your teaching ability in this area.

In this entry, the key elements are how the library media specialist demonstrates expertise in the use of technology in instruction, and how he or she models and fosters the ethical use of information. The entry specifically notes that accomplished library media specialists do the following.

Know how to match students and information. This skill is based partly on the use of the reference interview, a skill usually covered in library science education coursework. The reference interview requires a delicate interaction between librarian and patron to find the best information for the patron, in the right format, and that exactly meets the patron's needs. Achieving this means that there can be no barriers between students and information. If a poor reading student needs to understand the geography of Australia, perhaps a video may be the best format. The answer that students are not allowed to check out videos, and worse, that the videos are kept locked in a back room for the use of a particular teacher, would not speak well for a candidate's entry.

Teach the use of technology by using technology. A graduate student once complained about having to sit through a three-hour lecture on constructivism. By the same token, school library media specialists who use overheads to teach web design may fall victim to the same unimaginative strategy. We show that we can teach critical thinking skills by requiring their use in the development of our own teaching strategies.

Educate; don't punish. The school library media specialist as copyright warden is never a pretty sight. Our role is to educate the school community about legal and ethical information issues, not to intrude on the intellectual and academic freedom of our teaching peers. Still, for all our talk about legal and ethical issues such as copyright, plagiarism, and privacy, we rarely use the power of the library-as-classroom to make sure that students follow these guidelines. It is imperative for this entry that we do that.

School library media specialists should show clearly that they understand why using technology that is integrated into the instructional process is more important than technology tacked on as a motivational sidebar to the lesson. That understanding should be modeled in the instructional development of this entry. We are leaders in the integration of technology in our professional lives. We need to demonstrate that understanding.

School library media specialists need to know what they are talking about. Although we are the answer people for copyright, fair use, and other legal and ethical issues and guidelines, are we really up on the current status of the law? When no one else in the building knows anything about a subject, it is sometimes easy to fall back on old knowledge. School library media specialists will have to realize that this entry will most likely be read by someone who knows the current status of information ethics. The information that is disseminated in our instruction must be accurate.

This entry is based on standards 1, 2, 3, 4, 5, 7, and 9, as noted in figure 11-1. *Remember, the assessment is based on the standards, not on the portfolio entry instructions.*

WHAT DO I SEND IN?

This entry also requires a videotape. For this entry, you must provide one videotape that contains two parts that are each ten minutes long. These must be from different parts of one instructional lesson. Like the videotape in the previous entry, you may stop the tape in between the segments, but not in the middle. Each ten-minute video part must be uninterrupted.

You will also write ten pages of commentary. You will have to write about what the assessors see on the videotape, talk about how you planned the instruction, and give your evaluation of the student learning that resulted. You will also send in up to four pages of instructional materials that you used during the lesson.

THE VIDEOTAPE

For this entry, you will need to prepare a twenty-minute videotape. This videotape will have two ten-minute segments showing different parts of a single

FIGURE 11-1 ■ *Standards Related to Entry Three*

STANDARD 1	***Knowledge of Learners***
	Accomplished library media specialists have knowledge of learning styles and of human growth and development.
STANDARD 2	***Knowledge of Teaching and Learning***
	Accomplished library media specialists know the principles of teaching and learning that contribute to an active learning environment.
STANDARD 3	***Knowledge of Library and Information Studies***
	Accomplished library media specialists know the principles of library and information studies needed to create effective, integrated library media programs.
STANDARD 4	***Integrating Instruction***
	Accomplished library media specialists integrate information literacy through collaboration, planning, implementation, and assessment of learning.
STANDARD 5	***Leading Innovation through the Library Media***
	Accomplished library media specialists lead in providing equitable access to and effective use of technologies and innovations.
STANDARD 7	***Reflective Practice***
	Accomplished library media specialists engage in reflective practice to increase their effectiveness.
STANDARD 9	***Ethics, Equity, and Diversity***
	Accomplished library media specialists uphold professional ethics and promote equity and diversity.

lesson. The definition of time between the segments has received some discussion. Some candidates have asked whether this means that the lesson can be continued over several days with the same class, or whether the definition of a single lesson with a single class means that both segments must come from the same time period. One candidate reported having the children change shirts for the second segment so that it would look like it was on a separate day. Others insisted that both taping segments were to be from the same day of instruction.

This is a perfect example of a question that should be answered by NBPTS. Even if a candidate reports a direct conversation with someone at the NBPTS office, the context between two similar situations could be different enough to generate a different answer from NBPTS for someone else.

It is probably best not to play games with the assessors. Instruction must be fresh and stimulating. Tricks will only make the instruction look false. You should never plan instruction around the video. Plan the lesson first and then figure out which parts of it will be videotaped, or videotape the entire instruction and then figure out which parts demonstrate the required prompts best.

The purpose of the video is to show how you use technology in your teaching, and then how you help learners use technology in their learning. You must choose two ten-minute unedited segments that you feel portray this effectively.

There is a story about a candidate in another teaching field that required a similar video. The candidate mistakenly taped one twenty-minute lesson. Frantically, she called in the media specialists to help her make the tape look like it was two separate segments. Read the directions, but don't try to fool the assessors. It's not worth trying to achieve a small gain and ending up making the entire entry unscorable.

"Videotape early and videotape often" is very good advice. Several hours of videotape may make it easy to pick out the two segments from a single lesson that best fit the needs of this entry.

WHAT DO I HAVE TO WRITE?

The written commentary for this entry should be no more than ten pages. As with the other entries, the length for each section is suggested.

Section One: Instructional Context (One Page)

As in the other entries, the first section of the written commentary is the instructional context. Again, this section asks for information about the school and class, the students, their characteristics and exceptionalities, and other areas of the teaching context.

The teaching context, in this setting, would probably include the technology available in the library, as well as the overall collection and resources available with which to integrate those technologies. For instance, if the school possesses wireless laptops that are usually used for instruction, that would be important, as well as the resources available to support that technology. It is crucial to give the assessor any information regarding the physical context of the library media center and its technologies. If teaching is being conducted in the computer lab, it would be important to note the location of the lab in relation to the library.

The prompt regarding particular instructional challenges may also be slightly different in this entry. In discussing technology, the students' comfort level may be a factor. If there is a range of comfort levels, that is extremely important, and may guide your choice of instructional strategies. It could be that the community context is important as well. The amount of technology to which students have access at home or in the community may be a strong factor in your instruction.

Section Two: Planning and Teaching Analysis (Seven Pages)

As with entry two, this section of the written commentary is based on the videotape entry. You should be experienced by now at answering questions regarding instructional goals, learning styles, interests, exceptionalities, and needs. Some of the questions, however, may be difficult to answer.

For most candidates, the most difficult prompt is the one asking for evidence that your students understood the effective use of technology in the learning process. We often teach how to use technology, but we rarely make sure that students know the definition of *effectiveness* in the use of that technology. Discussion in the school library media literature centers on ways that technology is effective, and on teaching technology skills to students. Teaching students not just how to select information technology, but going further to have students analyze the ways that technology was and was not effective is not covered as thoroughly. There has to be an assessment mechanism that can show that students grasp the concept of effective use of technology. This is not an easy thing to show.

Other prompts requiring additional thought are the following.

Enhancement of the students' knowledge of legal and ethical issues. We do teach this in the school library field, but we don't always track the students' knowledge of legal or ethical issues. We don't use language such as *identity theft, right to privacy, fair use*, or *copyright infringement*, but these concepts may be embedded in subtle points in the lesson. These concepts must be more overt in this lesson.

Why were certain resources or technologies selected? Teaching the use of technology as an information tool means that there are specific ways in which certain technologies are used best. If students get to choose which final product to produce for assessment purposes, it is probably a good idea to discuss the ways that you guided their choices. This gets close in some ways to usability studies: researching, for instance, the reasons to choose a paper versus an electronic product, or choosing PowerPoint over a series of linked web pages. There is a reason, and it may be situated in the comfort level of the students, plus their learning styles. Background reading in how and why technology users make these choices may be needed to incorporate those concepts in the student instructional objectives.

Section Three: Reflection (Two Pages)

Again, as in the previous entry, a separate section is included for reflection. Remember that in this entry's planning and analysis section, you should have adequately described the planning and teaching. In this section, the attention is turned to the larger picture. Were the learning goals met? Was the lesson a success? Could it have been improved?

Remember in this section to review the learning goals as they pertain to the objective of this entry. You were integrating technology as part of your goals, so those will necessarily have to be part of the assessment. Integration of technology is the purpose of this entry. The integration has to be overt and complete.

Another part of this section asks how the lesson will influence future instruction. We rarely think in the school library field about the concept of "scaffolding," but it is certainly a part of what we do. In other subject fields, material is officially scaffolded by grade level. The skills of third-grade science build on the skills of second-grade science, and lead to the future skills of fourth-grade science.

The scaffolding of the library media field is different. There is a diverse body of knowledge and skills that students bring with them in the use of technology that has more to do with previous access than with previous formal training. Students may know how to do a task, but they may not know why, or they may not know the legal or ethical boundaries that surround that task. If all students are to make an equal amount of learning progress, then the instruction must take into account these varied pre-experiences.

Most of what students have previously learned about technology takes place out of school, and away from permanent records or other assessments. There is no way to know the skill level of the students, or the depth of the knowledge behind their skills. It is easier to see what they do, but that is iceberg learning. We have to delve a little deeper to be accomplished teachers of library media.

INSTRUCTIONAL MATERIALS

Again, as with the literature entry, you are permitted to send up to four pages of instructional materials. It is probably a good idea to take screenshots of areas that you are visiting on the Web, especially if they are focal points for instruction. You may also want to sketch out overheads or writing on the board. If you are asking the class to draw and complete a graphic organizer, for example, it may be helpful to sketch these out.

The videotape, although it must be uninterrupted, can swing from the students to zoom in on a chalk- or whiteboard. However, think of what the assessors need in front of them to ensure that they understand the lesson. Since you are limited in the number of pages that can be sent with the entry, make sure you are sending materials that enhance the video, rather than duplicating what the assessors have already seen.

SUMMARY

This entry will show your ability to integrate technology into the teaching process. In this entry, school library media specialists must exemplify the exact opposite of the classroom teacher using the Friday afternoon video. Closing the blinds on Friday after lunch, putting in an instructional video, then going to the back of the room to grade papers is a very poor example of the use of technology in schools.

This entry is a way to show the field the best use of technology integrated into the instructional life of the school. We need to show technology so tightly integrated into the teaching process that it is impossible to pull out and stand alone. In true integration, the technology use will be weakened without the strong context of the content lesson, and the content will lose the enhancement that technology brings. It is the perfect marriage of convenience: a win-win situation that strengthens classroom instruction, provides an opportunity to teach information skills, and gives students the skills they need for lifelong information use.

Food for Thought

Are you teaching the use of technologies or are you teaching the effective use of technologies? Sometimes those lines blur. It may help to write reflectively after lessons in which you have integrated technology. Questions such as "What did this lesson teach?" "How did technology further those skills?" and "Was technology necessary to this instructional process?" may help to identify lessons in which the effective use of technology was most directly employed.

An important part of this lesson is the teaching of information ethics. This should not be an add-on, but is most likely integrated into every lesson. When planning lessons involving technology, identify those times when you have stressed the integrity of information authorship, privacy, and other ethical principles. If those are under the surface of your teaching, you may want to make them more obvious.

NOTE

1. National Board for Professional Teaching Standards, *Early Childhood through Young Adulthood: Library Media: Scoring Guide* (Arlington, VA: National Board for Professional Teaching Standards, 2004), 32.

Entry Four: Documented Accomplishments

The first three portfolio entries are unique to the school library media teaching NBPTS process. However, the fourth entry, Documented Accomplishments, is the same across NBPTS entries in all teaching fields. In this entry, accomplished teachers show how their leadership in the school, the professional arena, and the community has impacted positively on student learning. Reaching out beyond students to their families is very important, along with involving colleagues such as teachers, administrators, and other libraries and librarians.

Because this entry is so different from the other three, the approach to preparing it is different as well. Some candidates find that this entry is the first one they tackle, since it looks at what has been accomplished in the past rather than in the present. Others find it easier to work on this entry periodically, as almost a break in between the other entries.

Documented Accomplishments concentrates on the improvement of instruction through professional growth activities. It shows the chain reaction of professional activities, professional growth, improvement of instruction, and benefit to students. This entry is a little shorter than the others, and it does not rely on the design or delivery of instruction

Clear, consistent, and convincing evidence of the teacher's ability to impact student learning through work with colleagues, professionals, families, and the community, and as a learner.[1]

141

through teaching an instructional unit. Instead, the entry focuses on the accomplished teacher as a conduit for professional growth in the school. The emphasis is not on personal professional growth, but rather on how the accomplished teacher has used personal professional growth to impact student learning in the entire school.

A common error on this entry is to make it a résumé, with everything that you have accomplished relating to what NBPTS refers to as being a learner and a leader/collaborator. Candidates who carefully document isolated service as a leader in their professional association, presentations at conferences, workshops attended and conducted, or services such as PTA liaison or school webmaster will not score well. These activities will not be impressive unless the candidate is able to draw a clear link between them and student learning, and through student learning to the community outside the doors of the library media center and of the school.

This is not to say that there are professional activities that have little meaning, or that some activities mean more than others. Every accomplishment can have an impact on student learning. If you have been president of your state school library affiliate, or active in the AASL, you must show how these activities provided you with learning, skills, experiences, or confidence that made a difference to students in your school and enabled you to plan activities that included the larger learning community. You can most likely show how those activities have had a direct impact on students, such as making a change in the way that you teach, or how the new leadership skills you are learning made it possible for you to take the lead in implementing new structures, routines, or technologies in the school library media program. The line can then be drawn from those changes to their direct impact on the structures, routines, and technologies of classroom learning.

This impact can also be indirect, such as conducting professional development workshops for the other teachers in the school so that they were able to change their instruction. You could also show how you inspired school library media specialists in other schools to do the same, therefore spreading the positive impact throughout the district. Change is therefore vertical, spreading from you to the classroom teachers, and horizontal, spreading sideways through the districts to library media specialists in other schools.

WHAT WILL I NEED TO DO?

The important points in this entry are the following.

Staff development programs. School library media specialists both deliver and attend staff development programs on a regular basis. More than in any other teaching field, the design of staff development workshops is seen as an important part of what we do.

Networking. Our ability to create linkages with other schools, other types of libraries, and community organizations is another hallmark of our field. School library media specialists, although they work alone in the school, are only as isolated as they choose to be. Conferences, electronic discussion lists, and professional associations are just some of the ways in which accomplished school library media specialists seek continuous professional growth.

Passion for the mission. The mission of the school library media program in the school, according to *Information Power*, is "to ensure that students and staff are effective users of ideas and information."[2] That mission requires a passionate belief in school libraries. The field has always had enthusiastic zealots who changed the face of school library media almost singlehandedly. Accomplished school library media specialists actively assume these roles.

This entry is based on standards 7, 8, and 10, as noted in figure 12-1. *Remember, the assessment is based on the standards, not on the portfolio entry instructions.*

The instructions for this entry have specific time periods in which accomplishments must have occurred. It might be wise to start with itemized lists of accomplishments and then make a timeline. The wording can be a little scary in this entry, using phrases such as "partner with student families." You may have to think for a while about the ways in which these accomplishments have had the impact that the NBPTS assessors will want to see. The impacts of the accomplishments most likely do exist. You have made an impact in the lives of students because very little of what educators do in their professional or even personal lives is separate from their lives as teachers. Those linkages are just not regularly identified or evaluated so that we can know and articulate the impact

FIGURE 12-1 ■ *Standards Related to Entry Four*

STANDARD 7	*Reflective Practice*
	Accomplished library media specialists engage in reflective practice to increase their effectiveness.
STANDARD 8	*Professional Growth*
	Accomplished library media specialists model a strong commitment to lifelong learning and to their profession.
STANDARD 10	*Leadership, Advocacy, and Community*
	Accomplished library media specialists advocate for the library media program, involving the greater community.

that school library media as a profession has on schoolwide and community-wide achievement and lifelong learning.

Try using a form similar to figure 12-2 to keep revising your list of activities. You may see that your list of accomplishments has several themes, perhaps literature, or technology, or another instructional area. You are allowed to provide documentation of a maximum of eight accomplishments in three categories. These categories are the following:

■ as a partner with students' families and their community during the current school year

■ as a learner (within the last five years)

■ as a leader/collaborator (within the last five years)

As a partner with students' families and their community during the current school year. As an exercise, make a list of the ways that you interact with students' families. Some librarians have done this by cooperating with the public library in a library card campaign, by having family story hours, or by hosting technology workshops. The basic question is this: "During the current year, how have you interacted with students' families?" The ways could be formal programs such as those just mentioned, or informal activities such as notes or letters sent home to parents.

Regardless of whether the interaction is a formalized program or an occasional activity, the communication should be two-way. A blanket memo sent home in students' book bags will either be read or not read, but how will you know the reaction of families to the communication? There must be a feedback loop built into the communication cycle. As with the communication, the feedback loop can be formal or informal. If you have had parents comment casually to you about the school library, you may be able to document the results of your interaction through letters of support for your candidacy, or by asking the PTA

FIGURE 12-2 ■ *Activity/Accomplishment Chart*

ACTIVITY/ACCOMPLISHMENT	TIME PERIOD	IMPACT ON STUDENT LEARNING

president to sign a documentation form noting the activities that you have conducted and confirming the parents' response to them.

As a learner (within the last five years). Most school library media specialists will have long lists of learning activities within the last five years. They may have attended state or national conferences, attended preconference workshops, engaged in professional growth activities at the school or district level, or even obtained graduate credit. Remember, however, that you must link those activities back to the student learning level. Figure 12-2 might be a good way to organize your learning activities in this category as well, so that you can see which ones have had the greatest impact on student learning.

As a leader/collaborator (within the last five years). Have you been a member or chair of a school, community, or professional association committee? Have you presented at conferences, held offices, or in some other way acted in a leadership role? Remember, though, that the accomplishments you choose must have either a direct or indirect impact on student learning.

For educators with a long list of accomplishments, deciding which ones to use for this entry is important. It is possible to have a coordinating theme, such as technology, or reading encouragement, or even the institutionalization of a particular learning style. For instance, the schoolwide initiative All Kinds of Minds may be your theme. You may have attended conference sessions (learner), represented your school at training sessions (learner, leader), or worked on a committee to investigate the best way to implement it (community, learner, leader). You may have received extra workshop training to become a trainer for your school (leader, learner) and conducted workshops for parents, the community, and the other teachers (community, leader).

Remember, though, to make the impact on student learning as overt as you can. Assessors must see that there is an obvious link to student achievement. This does not mean test scores, necessarily, but the assessors must believe that increased learning could be expected to result from your activities.

The question of whether or not to submit less than eight accomplishments is a difficult choice. You may feel that your portfolio entry is solid, that you have documented student learning, and that you have adequately covered each and every point. You may want to discuss this with NBPTS and a few school library media NBCTs to see if you can make a decision. It may well be that you decide that including a literature-based professional accomplishment will strengthen this entry, since your other accomplishments may be technology-based. Or you may decide that it is best to appear well-rounded by including professional accomplishments that are wide-ranging and cover all of the roles of the school library media specialist. You may wonder which of your professional accomplishments will be looked at with the most favor by NBPTS, and try to create a ranked list of accomplishments.

There are no correct answers to this question. The advice that candidates receive from other candidates or from NBCTs is always suspect, but never more so than in this entry. The entry is based on how candidates show their commitment to student learning in a unique library media center based in a unique school and in a unique community. Even those candidates who were very successful in this entry were successful in another context, which can be thought of as another planet: that of their own school library program. Talk to candidates, talk to the National Board, but the decision of how to approach this entry has to be yours alone.

Like much of the NBPTS process, your professional judgment about your entries must be the basis for what you decide to do. Rely on the scoring guide for the exact rubrics and prompts and try to think as much like an assessor as possible, so that you can make good decisions about the process.

WHAT DO I SEND IN?

All of the documentation supporting your accomplishments is in written form. You will have three types of written documentation: the Description and Analysis section, the Documentation, and a Reflective Summary.

Section One: Description and Analysis (Ten Pages)

The key words in this entry are "what, why, and how." This description section is not one story but rather is multilayered, with subplots for each of the areas in which candidates must show competence (partnerships with students' families and the community, growth as a learner, and experiences as an educational leader). You may choose to document a total of eight accomplishments as evidence for these three areas.

Some candidates choose to group their accomplishments by category, to show that they have covered each of the areas. Others group the entry by accomplishment, so that each accomplishment may address one or more of the categories. Regardless of the method used, candidates are limited to ten pages of description and analysis.

You must first describe the accomplishment, making sure that the assessor knows enough about your teaching context to understand the nature of the accomplishment completely. Next you will describe why the accomplishment is significant, and finally, how it impacts student learning.

Note that you will be describing and analyzing the eight accomplishments in a maximum of ten pages. It will be difficult not to sound redundant by the eighth accomplishment. For this reason alone, it may be wise to keep coming back to this entry, perhaps when you experience writer's block on the others. As you become a more experienced candidate, you may change some of the writing as you see more clearly the ways that your work impacts the learning of students in your school.

You will probably decide at some point along the way to completely reorganize this entry, perhaps several times. There may be a point at which you must declare this entry finished. Because of the open nature of the prompts, and the variety of ways in which candidates can choose to address the requirements, it is tempting to keep revising this entry until the very end. This entry is not worth as much as the other portfolio entries, however. Time spent on the others may be more valuable in the end.

Section Two: Documentation (Sixteen Pages)

You are allowed sixteen pages of documentation to support the eight accomplishments that you choose to select. Although mathematically this results in two pieces of documentation per accomplishment, that may not be the best solution. Three types of documentation are permissible: artifacts, verification forms, and communication logs.

It may be that one artifact, such as a flyer announcing a staff development workshop you are conducting or an award as teacher of the year for your building, may be sufficient to prove an accomplishment in a specific area. For other accomplishments, you may need to use a communication log to show communication with parents, a verification letter from the PTA president, and a copy of a newsletter article for the PTA.

The entry instructions give detailed directions for the preparation of documentation. As with all of the entries, pay careful attention to what you are and are not allowed to send. A great accomplishment may be meaningless if the documentation was not usable.

Section Three: Reflective Summary (Two Pages)

In two pages you will not have enough time to review each accomplishment. Rather, this summary should look at these accomplishments as a whole, and should review their effectiveness. Think of this section as a stopping place on a path. You are being asked to turn around, look behind you, and reflect on the accomplishments that had the greatest impact on student learning. You are then asked to turn back to the road in front of you, and reflect on your future accomplishments. This will mean evaluating the pattern of your accomplishments and then projecting that pattern into the future. Your plans to impact student learning in the future, and the processes that you choose to implement those plans, will be that basis of your reflection.

Accomplished library media specialists have an opinion about the needs of the students in their school, and they are able to articulate how they can play a part in meeting those needs.

SUMMARY

This entry asks you to choose eight accomplishments in three areas: teacher as partner with families and community, teacher as learner, and teacher as collaborator. Of these three categories, the last two are integral to best practices for a school library media specialist. It is perhaps harder for us as a field to make partnering connections with parents and the community. We may feel that the school is too big, or our meetings with students too fleeting, to make effective connections. Still, our accomplishments in this area can show, more than anything else, the direct connection that we have with student achievement.

Candidates at times try to devise a project to show accomplishments in one of these areas. Although certainly the work of the school library media center must continue despite the attention that the NBPTS process requires from you, this entry will score highest when candidates can prove a *pattern* of documented accomplishments. School library media specialists work as the hub of the school, literally turning the spokes that make up the educational processes in the school and the community. At first thought, no accomplishments that fit this area may come to mind, but over time, accomplished library media specialists can weave together their past experiences, awards, and activities to show how they achieve the requirements of this entry.

This entry is sometimes the one that candidates look at first when they are thinking about applying for National Board certification. Some career paths lead both to and occasionally away from professional activity. A multiyear hiatus in your professional development activities will not provide many details for this entry. The fact that you were very active six years ago is irrelevant. It is possible to gear up for this entry by increasing your documented accomplishments over time.

It is also easy to miss your greatest strength. Ask your students, other teachers, and your family what they think your greatest accomplishment is. Their answer will be what they have noticed you consider to be your greatest passion. You can write a lot about what you love. There is no ranked list of accomplishments. This is an opportunity for you to write about what you consider to be your greatest impact on the lives of your school community.

> ## Food for Thought
>
> Juggling three categories and eight accomplishments may start to feel like doing a complex jigsaw puzzle. Use different colored highlighters to ensure that you have each category covered as thoroughly as the rubric requires.
>
> Ask an educator and at least one person not in the education field to read this entry. When they finish, ask them how they think you have impacted student learning. You may be surprised at their interpretation of points that you thought were very clear.

NOTES

1. National Board for Professional Teaching Standards, *Early Childhood through Young Adulthood: Library Media: Scoring Guide* (Arlington, VA: National Board for Professional Teaching Standards, 2004), 38.
2. American Association of School Librarians, Association for Educational Communications and Technology, *Information Power: Building Partnerships for Learning* (Chicago: American Library Association, 1998), 7.

13 Assessment Center Exercises

It's over. The box is finished and sitting on the dining room table. Everything has been packed, repacked, and double-checked by several people, and it is complete. It is ready to be mailed, and has been ready for three days. So why is it still sitting on the table?

The person who first defined *separation anxiety* probably was a National Board candidate. It may help to think not of finishing the portfolio entries, but rather of abandoning them. You might get a better score if you were able to rewrite the entries one more time, to look over the documented accomplishments just to make sure that you covered all of the categories, or to time the videos again just to check that they are scorable. But you are not going to do that. It's time to mail the box. You have worked endless hours, declared the dining room off-limits for three months now, and have not slept soundly in the last two weeks.

Just mail it.

The electronic discussion lists are rife with humorous stories about mailing the box. The person whose fingers had to be pried off the box by the mail room clerk. The one who took a bevy of friends with her to mail it. The one who hid on the floor of the car while her spouse mailed it. Tracking the box as it makes its way across the country also allows for extra anxious moments, and candidates regularly report on its progress.

The anxiety that assails candidates about mailing the box probably has been increased by the length of time it took to pack it, double-check its contents, and pack it again. This is not the same as packing for a weekend trip. The individual number of pieces, including bar codes, may be far more than you expected. Some candidates prefer to pack as they go. When they know they have finished an entry, they label and pack it, periodically adding to their sense of accomplishment. Periodically, as you did with the inventory when you received the box, you can unpack and repack it again, checking once more that all of the contents are there. Soon, however, it has to leave your hands and begin its trip to being assessed.

The sense of doom that releasing this precious cargo can bring is soon replaced by a sense of dread. The assessment center exercises will come fast on the heels of the portfolio entries. One of the first important tasks that will have to be accomplished is to set the date for taking the assessment center exercises. This date cannot be changed, so thinking through how this date interacts with your life is important.

When we teach our students, we usually abide no excuses. Forget your assignment? Ten points off. Forget your pencil? Lose your notebook? Miss a deadline? All of these have dire consequences for students, as we tell ourselves that we are teaching them responsibility. In the adult world, however, none of those consequences apply. Forgetting to have supplies, losing things, all of these events are expected occasionally, and the world makes the necessary allowances for them and moves on. Only the most obsessive person would expect that not having a writing instrument at all times is worthy of strict punishment, either for themselves or for another.

The assessment center, however, is one place where consequences do exist. Once the date is set it cannot be changed, and there is a window of time when it has to occur. There have been events reported on the discussion lists such as a severe illness requiring intensive chemotherapy, the sudden death of a loved one, or car accidents requiring hospital stays. In other circumstances, each of these situations might allow for some accommodation and the date may be changed. But it is the strict adherence to deadlines that makes the NBPTS process so fair. You set the test center date, and you will arrange your life accordingly. So will everyone else in the room.

Once you register for the date, broadcast it to all your friends and relatives. No parties, marriages, babies, vacations, or any other event can take place in a broad window leading up to that date. There have been some announcements that "I just finished the assessment center exercises, we're off to Disney World," and that may be a great idea as a stress reliever and a celebration for the family.

Just leave the planning for the trip to someone else. You cannot spend your time making hotel reservations, planning cruises, and double-checking flights. You have work to do.

You will be signing up for a series of tests in which you have to demonstrate your knowledge of the best practices in the school library field. You have already demonstrated evidence of your teaching practices and have come a long way in this process. You are almost there, but you have to study.

THE ASSESSMENT CENTER

When you register and are assigned to a testing center, your first step should be to find out as much as you can about the physical character of the center. Does it have cubicles or flat desks? Will I be able to take tissues with me? What is the noise level? And of course, the obvious: where is it, and where can I park?

Gear your studying around the physical setting of the assessment center. Your knowledge will not do you any good if you are studying in complete silence with a serene view, and then you find yourself having to type in a small room shoulder-to-shoulder with strangers, some of whom have nervous habits such as pencil-tapping, teeth grinding, or heaven forbid, humming. Re-create the physical setting of the assessment center. If you are easily distracted, then study while watching TV with the family to build up your concentration skills.

Some states with active mentoring groups conduct study sleepovers where candidates report in, assessment areas are assigned, and there are handouts for everyone. Of course, each person is responsible for all of the content, but having someone locate good sources and the best articles and reading materials is a big help.

One asset that you are not permitted to use is information from past candidates. Although NBCTs frequently mentor, help you study pertinent information, and prepare you for the rigors of the assessment, they cannot give you confidential information about the assessment exercises themselves. They have signed a confidentiality agreement, and asking them for information they have sworn not to give puts their certification in jeopardy.

THE EXERCISES

There are six assessment center exercises. Each one presents a topic and then a scenario, and asks a question based on the scenario; in most cases this question consists of two parts. Most advice from previous test-takers is to change screens to look at both parts, and then begin answering the question. The candidate has thirty minutes in which to give a written response to the question. The six exercises are on the topics of organizational management, ethical and legal tenets, technologies, collection development, information literacy, and knowledge of literature.

Think of each test as knowledge first, then application of that knowledge. You cannot score well if you do only the knowledge part and never get to the application section.

Organizational Management

In the organizational management exercise, you will have to demonstrate that you have knowledge of administrative issues in the library media center and of how to solve problems. You will be given a scenario and have to identify the issues, analyze possible solutions, and then propose strategies.

You may think that simply by running a library every day you have achieved enough organizational expertise to be able to do this entry. You may, but you will need to refresh yourself on the management practices by name. Dig back through your closet and find your school library administration text, or check one out from a nearby university library. Skim the issues and make study notes. The key to this entry is to know the best practices of the field as they relate to the management of the school library. Make lists of broad management issues such as planning, budgeting, personnel management of library clerks or volunteers, and others. You may know what to do in any scenario that you devise, but you also have to know why it is considered best practice to do that.

Information Power details the mission and vision of the school library, and outlines the principles underlying the program administration role.[1] It will be important to be able to articulate these principles. Some candidates have found it helpful to memorize the principles so that they can always have them as a guide in their reading.

Educational administration texts such as those used in the preparation of school administrators may be helpful as well, and can be found in any college bookstore offering those courses. Those volumes will address Maslow's need hierarchy, Herzberg's motivation theories, and other management topics from the business world that may be helpful.

One journal of interest is *Library Administration and Management*, published by the ALA's Library Administration and Management Association. This journal, although addressed primarily to public, special, and academic libraries, covers management topics that you can apply to the school library field.

On the practical level, begin to recognize possible questions in the day-to-day operation of your library. As a school library media specialist in an active school library, you may make dozens of management decisions each day. You observe the situation, draw from your experience, weigh the evidence, and test possible solutions, developing and discarding possibilities until you exercise professional judgment to make a choice between the viable options.

This process may take only seconds, and most of it may occur at the subconscious level. You may have to consciously apply reflective writing practices to describe, analyze, and reflect on a particular case. Each day, can you pick out one instance in which you made a management decision, and can you articulate the decision-making process for it?

Ethical and Legal Tenets

This exercise is by far the most specific one. Although there are many ethical and legal tenets in the library field that could have possibly been chosen, this exercise specifically mentions the intellectual freedom area. You will be asked to describe the process of reconsideration of materials, and then describe a professional resource that would be helpful in that process and explain its value.

The documents you may need for this challenge can be found at the Office for Intellectual Freedom's home page on the ALA website. Another good place to start on that website is the "Intellectual Freedom" section under the AASL Resource Guides.[2] You may want to read in the professional literature some articles dealing with the reconsideration of materials. This is a well-documented area; and the steps to take when the censor arrives at your doorstep, what materials and documents you should have at hand, and advocacy suggestions to avoid challenges in the first place can all be found at the ALA's Office for Intellectual Freedom web pages. You may also want to review the literature on the selection process in general.

The degree to which intellectual freedom was reviewed in school library media preparation classes may rest on geographic factors. In areas where challenges are common, such as Virginia and North Carolina, a great deal of time may have been spent in preparing for challenges and reviewing procedures to be followed. Professional conferences may have at least one session on intellectual freedom issues each year, and discussion lists and casual conversations include mention of schools and districts with ongoing challenges to materials.

In other states challenges may be rare, and the documents and processes involved in the reconsideration of materials may be mentioned only briefly as part of an administration text, and not discussed at all in class. In that case, there may be some background reading that is essential. It may also be helpful to talk to several school library media specialists who have experienced challenges. Until you have been through a challenge, it is hard to know the importance of the right steps and the best documentation.

Technologies

Sometimes librarians feel that they have to choose between technology and reading, as if the library field were engaged in playing the child's game Red

Rover, Red Rover on a giant scale. Perhaps you are one of the many school library media specialists who can play on either side with equal skill, and frequently show your expertise in both areas.

More often, though, school library media specialists consider themselves to be more skilled at one than the other. Although you may consider that you are comfortable in both reading and technology, this exercise may challenge you. You will have to demonstrate knowledge in three areas: hardware, software, and connectivity. You will be given a specific objective, and then will need to accomplish that objective and explain the technological needs.

A useful review for this objective may be to ask the computer facilitator in your school and district for a list of journals. Certainly *Tech Trends* or *Multimedia and Internet @ Schools* may be helpful. The technology sections of popular journals such as *Library Media Connection* (formerly *Book Report*) may be helpful as well.[3]

In preparing for each of the exercises, you may want to make up questions to answer, but especially for this exercise. You may not only want to have your answers vetted by someone you consider to be strong in these three areas (hardware, software, connectivity), but you might also want the questions that you come up with to be reviewed, so you can be sure that you fully understand the topic.

Lunch conversation with your school's technology director may be worth your time as well. Ask questions, but more importantly, ask and answer your own questions, then listen to the way that the technology director answers them. Every field has its own jargon and lexicon. Phrasing your answer correctly may be as important as the content that you know.

Collection Development

Lillian Gearhart, one-time editor of *School Library Journal*, once praised the selection process as the most important skill of a librarian. While this assertion is perhaps a bit overdone, still it is true that selection and collection development are the heart of our profession. In almost all library schools, there will be an entire course devoted to this topic, and many good basic texts are available.[4]

Candidates should be aware of the basic principles of selection and should also know the basics of building a collection development plan, along with a plan for promoting new acquisition. Because of the area of promotion of the new acquisition that is included with this question, candidates should have at least a casual knowledge of advocacy principles in libraries. Fortunately, there is much information about advocacy available on the AASL home page. The "Professional Tools" area contains downloadable brochures and toolkits that may be helpful.[5]

Information Literacy

In this exercise, candidates must have a knowledge of information literacy processes and will then have to apply that knowledge in a scenario. Some of the more widely used information skills processes are Kuhlthau's Information Search Process, Eisenberg and Berkowitz's Big6 skills, I-search, Follett's Pathways to Knowledge, and Stripling and Pitts's mental models. (See the "Further Reading" section in chapter 3 for recommended reading in this area.) One strategy for studying is to make flash cards of each step in each process, and be able to relate those steps back to instructional theories. For instance, can you apply Kuhlthau's ISP or I-search to a constructivist or a mastery learning philosophy?

For confidence in this exercise, candidates should be able—given a grade level, topic, and class description—to pick an information skills instructional strategy, review the steps that would be applied, and discuss what they would expect to see at each step. This requires some degree of memorization, but also a bit of application and wide reading. As in most of the assessment center exercises, some of the knowledge background needed has already been required for the portfolio entries. The notes from your portfolio entries, as you wrote about your instructional methodologies at that time, will be very helpful.

You should be able to understand and explain the best-known research skill processes, when to teach them, and what their steps are, along with how to implement them in a given situation at any grade level.

Knowledge of Literature

This assessment center exercise is perhaps the most talked about of any of them. Picture yourself in the assessment center. You have already written five of the thirty-minute exercises. On some of these, you felt confident, and were able to rest your fingers before the end of the allotted time. On others, you know that your score will not be strong. Your brain is numb, and you have been sitting for nearly three hours. You begin the last exercise with a sigh.

A book will appear before you on the screen. You will have to apply selection criteria used in evaluating literature, and you will have to apply that literary work to enrich a content lesson.

In the worst-case scenario, you do not recognize any of the books. Don't panic. Remember what you do know. You can discuss the criteria used in evaluating any piece of literature, and you can discuss the steps you would use to apply any piece of literature to a content lesson. You will at least gain some points. Yes, this would be a low-scoring entry in that situation, but remember that you only have to average 2.75 points out of a possible 4. You do not have to score 2.75 on every entry.

Another reason for the attention given this exercise is the identifiably wide age range for the literature that could possibly be chosen. It is wise to keep in mind that the same wide age range of 3–18 years applies to every exercise, not just literature. In literature, the age range can simply be applied to specific materials.

There are many book lists available for use in preparing for this entry. Certainly the award-winning books from the ALA should be chosen, including Newbery, Caldecott, Coretta Scott King, Pura Belpré, and the ALA notables. Review the list of authors from the lifetime achievement awards to make sure that you did not miss any of the Laura Ingalls Wilder authors. The list of the awards in chapter 6 will be helpful.

Some candidates have used books on tape or CD to maximize their reading time. A twenty-minute commute twice a day can provide a lot of listening time. Regardless of your method of preparation, remember that you not only have to know the book, but also know how it could be used in collaboration with a classroom teacher in a subject area. Set up a note card system from your reading, recording on each card the answers to the questions required in the exercise (evaluation criteria, how you would use the book to enrich a content curriculum).

PREPARING PHYSICALLY FOR THE EXERCISES

During the last round of the NBPTS process, while waiting for scores, an interesting discussion began on the library media electronic discussion list on the positives and negatives of food versus exercise as stress relief. Stories of pounds gained and lost, of brownies eaten and gyms joined, were attacked as seriously as any of the preparation questions.

Although at times humorous, physical preparation for the assessment center cannot be taken lightly. The physical act of answering each question is as important as knowledge, and the last question is as important as the first one was. You should be aware that by the time three hours have passed you will be brain dead, and your fingers will have to act on automatic pilot. But if you practice for this ordeal, you should be prepared for it.

First, schedule practice sessions in the weeks leading up to the assessment center exercises. You should expect to experience three hours of sitting at your computer typing. With a break in the middle, this probably comes out to an almost four-hour time block. Note the time of day that you will be taking this test. If you are not a morning person and you will be required to rise much earlier than usual to get to the center, you will have to practice that as well.

Re-create the scene as much as possible. If you cannot take any food or drink into the test area, do not have it at your computer. Some candidates had snacks that would be available, such as a specific vending machine snack, so that they could feel emotionally prepared ("When I get to the peanut butter crackers, I will be almost finished").

You will probably have questions prepared on cards on which to practice for each assessment center exercise. Every practice session, sit at your computer as if prepared for an assessment center exercise. Pull a card at random, breathe deeply, and begin typing the answer. Whenever possible, use the retired prompts available at the NBPTS website. This will make you feel that you are as close to the real experience as you can get.

Remember as well that you cannot discuss the theory and then solve the scenario. You have to tie the pieces together to make one picture. The phrase "grounded in the scenario" is a visual picture of a tree of theory blooming out of the ground of the scenario. That is hard for some candidates, since they may be used to keeping theory and practice separate. It is also probably wise to study the exercises in their actual order. You want your participation in the assessment center exercises to be as automatic as possible.

What is the worst-case scenario? The equipment freezes, you throw up over the computer keys, or the power goes out at the testing center. Mishaps like these occasionally happen, but if one does, fill out a report immediately at the testing center. Even if you were almost finished and you may decide that you really didn't lose that much information and you would like to think about it, you should fill out a report. Filing an appeal is expensive, but without the report at the time of the incident, you will not have the evidence that you need.

SUMMARY

Yogi Berra's comment "It ain't over till it's over" rings truer than ever for the assessment center portion of the NBPTS process. The portfolio entries are draining and will take all of your time and energy for several months. The relief you will feel upon getting the box out of your life may enervate you to the point that you will find it difficult to pick up the traces and continue on to study for the assessment center exercises. Still, they are out there and coming very quickly.

In some ways, the assessment center exercises are easier because they are just content knowledge with performance elements. Most of the questions are in areas that you may be able to identify as your areas of strength. On the other hand, teachers are notoriously bad at taking tests, ironic in a profession that focuses on assessment and grading. If you have test anxiety, it can ruin your chances of a good score. Set up mental triggers to relax, and practice the physical act of taking the tests. Your mind may refuse to function, but with practice, your body will take over and naturally move into the stream of enforced habits you have practiced.

Some candidates will say that the most difficult part of the process was neither the portfolio entries nor the assessment center exercises. The most difficult time for many candidates started when they left the door of the assessment center, and continued until they learned their scores. Waiting to learn whether or not you have achieved the coveted status of accomplished teacher is very difficult. Even more so is the fear of not achieving that status. You may relive each portfolio entry and each assessment center exercise, wondering what you scored.

A more productive activity at this time might be to think about what you learned from the NBPTS process. Keep writing and reflecting on your learning process. Although this will not make the waiting easier, it may help you to see the continuum of the National Board process not as an end, but rather as an important beginning to the next stage of your career.

Food for Thought

Read through the tables of contents for professional practitioner journals. Retrieve those articles that seem to match an assessment center exercise. You may want to abstract or outline the articles that seem to be most pertinent.

Study groups are a great idea in preparing for the assessment center. Each candidate in the group can take the responsibility for a specific journal or a specific entry and read and report back to the group. Think virtual. The group can be scattered across the country, or it can be local and still meet for weekly chats and e-mail reports.

NOTES

1. American Association of School Librarians, Association for Educational Communications and Technology, *Information Power: Building Partnerships for Learning* (Chicago: American Library Association, 1998).
2. The AASL Resource Guides has current resources on a variety of professional topics. Candidates may want to browse the entire list, but intellectual freedom issues can be found on the AASL website at http://www.ala.org/aaslTemplate.cfm?Section= resourceguides.
3. *Tech Trends* is the journal of the Association for Educational Communications and Technology.
4. The most commonly used text is probably Phyllis Van Orden, Kay Bishop, and Patricia Pawelak-Kort, *The Collection Program in Schools* (Englewood, CO: Libraries Unlimited, 2001).
5. The ALA website has a section on advocacy, but most candidates will want to go directly to the AASL Professional Tools section at http://www.ala.org/aaslTemplate .cfm?Section=aaslproftools.

14 Banking

Okay . . . now you truly are finished. You're done. The portfolio is sent off, the assessment center exercises are finished. It's over.

Now you wait. And wait. And wait.

Most candidates report that this period is the hardest part of the process. Candidates vying for the designation of accomplished teacher tend to be self-confident, strong-willed, and determined. You have done everything that you can do, and you are at the mercy of an organization that runs on its own timetable.

The scores will be posted on the announced day. They will not be posted until all portfolios and assessment exercises are graded. This is an equity issue. Can you imagine the anxiety if some scores were available and not others? Considering the amount of assessment that must be accomplished, the speed at which the grading occurs is amazing, even though candidates waiting to learn their fate might disagree with this statement.

The strategy for finding out your scores varies as well. Do you log on to check every hour? Or should you wait until you know that they are posted and other candidates have announced the good news? So you logged on, and you scanned the list. The $2,500 that you paid to take the test, the months of work, the time spent away from your family, and the anxious moments behind you all race through your mind as you scan once, twice, and a third time. Your name is not there. You check your scores, and it is true. You did not make the list of National Board Certified Teachers.

The chance that this is a mistake (yours or that of NBPTS) may be a first thought, but rationality soon takes over. You have received your scores, and you did not achieve the requisite 2.75 to pass. In your mind, you have failed.

BANKING

The NBPTS process is not a one-time test. As previously mentioned, you can choose to retain certain sections of the ten-part assessment on which you scored fairly high, and choose to redo other sections. This is called "banking," and the people who did not achieve NBCT status and are in the process of retaking the tests are sometimes called "bankers," although NBPTS refers to them as "retake candidates."

Banking is quite common in other rigorous assessment processes. The state bar exam for prospective lawyers and the CPA exam for accountants are two that come to mind immediately. Candidates for these exams note which sections they passed, and which sections they will sit for again.

Candidates in these exams, while certainly hoping that they pass the first time, will readily admit that they expected it to be a multiyear event. The rigor of the process ensures that there are some areas or topics that the candidate may not be comfortable with the first time. This is not seen as an embarrassing or humiliating problem, but more as a strategy to take the test the first time, get the more familiar and therefore higher-scoring sections finished, and then concentrate on those that will need more time for study.

Teachers are a different breed. Academic failure is not something that sits lightly on their shoulders. Teachers are in a business where success is determined by straight As. Teachers are successful products of the educational system which they reinforce on a daily basis. Calling oneself a banker or a retake candidate will take some time to get accustomed to. You possibly went into the process telling yourself, your family, colleagues, and peers that it is a four-year process, but you never thought this would apply to you.

Regardless of whether you refer to yourself as a continuing candidate, a banker, or a retake candidate, it is probably not the designation you wanted to achieve. You wanted to be an NBCT, and see those letters behind your name. You still can. You have to remember that this is a multiyear process, usually four years. You spent a year preparing and so you have just completed year one. Now you have to decide what you will do.

DECISION PATHWAYS

The first decision to make is not to make a decision. Step back and give yourself a day or two to not think about it. Be up-front and honest with students, parents, peers, and administrators. No, I did not make the requisite score, and I don't know what I am going to do. End of sentence and end of conversation. If the question is asked about your options, say that you are giving yourself two days before you think about options. You'll get back to them.

Stay in communication with others on the discussion lists, however. The first year that testing was offered, retake candidates were almost completely silent. Some candidates, very few, noted that they did not pass, did not understand why, and some withdrew from the list and from the process. The second year, though, the retake candidates came forth and announced their success proudly, and encouraged other retake candidates to do the same.

In the third year, NBCTs who had taken two years to achieve the successful 2.75 or higher score were active on the discussion lists before the scores were announced, preparing candidates for the chance that they would not be successful their first or even their second year. These "it happened to me and it worked out okay" stories were invaluable in encouraging candidates who scored low in some sections to ask questions regarding their possible errors or omissions.

Why?

We don't know a whole lot about why really good teachers do not always achieve NBCT status on their first try, their second try, or even on the third. The assessments require clear, consistent, and convincing evidence of accomplished teaching. Even though an assessor may see on the videotape that a candidate is an excellent teacher, unless the written materials provide the necessary evidence according to the scoring rubric, the entries will not score well.

Some insight can be gained by reading the discussion lists of teachers who reread their entries, sometimes with a mentor or an experienced NBCT. Some bankers noted that they clearly saw they did not meet the requirements of the rubric. Almost always this was detected not by them, but by an NBCT they had asked to read their entry. Even NBCTs in other subject areas were helpful in pointing out errors and omissions.

A surprising number of these candidates reported that their weakest scores came in areas that they thought were their strongest ones. Their confidence in these areas led them to disregard the rubric and instead just rely on their knowledge. In the areas that they felt less confident, they relied on the rubric and writing prompts entirely.

A handful reported physical or emotional reasons for not achieving NBCT status. Some reported a death or serious illness in the family, were ill themselves, or were simply too overwhelmed to complete the process as well as they knew they could.

Another small group had flaws in the logistics. They lost bar codes, had difficulties with the logistics of taping (e.g., no sound) or other problems. This group usually knew that they had an entry that would not score well, but they assumed, correctly, that they could redo that section the following year. Of course, some of these were successful. Even though they may have had an entry score very low, they may have had another entry score very high, and their overall average was strong enough to overcome the low points in one or two entries.

Retake candidates who were successful the following year were ready to assist candidates who confessed that their scores fell below the requisite 2.75. They shared their feelings openly, and many said how easy it was to only take several sections the following year instead of the entire ten-part assessment. This created more conversation on the discussion lists, making the banking candidates feel that what they perceived to be a failure was perhaps just a minor glitch, and one that they would get over.

When?

Step one is to find out the timeline for making the decision about whether to continue with the candidacy process or not. Usually, that will be in a month or two. Once you know that, set your own deadline several days before, by which time you will have made the decision to go ahead or not. Discuss the options openly, but don't try to arrive at a decision early. You may regret the missed opportunities for success that come from rushing the important decision.

Where?

Step two is to find out why your lowest-scoring entries did so poorly. You must have missed something somewhere. You need to be able to locate your errors or omissions. Ask an NBCT to read your entry, and ask a non-NBCT to read it as well. Trained assessors, regardless of whether they are NBCTs or whether they have experience working on other projects, will note that they have the scoring rubric at hand while they assess, and that they check it point by point. In a low-scoring entry, something that was supposed to be there was missing, and you have to figure out what that was.

Usually, when that happens, it will be glaringly apparent to you. The feelings of self-loathing and nonacceptance will be rampant. You missed something. It happens. Now pick yourself up and do it again.

If the mistake was due to a lack of knowledge in your background, you may want to contact a professor at the nearest school library media preparation program. Sometimes the entry can be pointed to a specific course, and you may want to look over the course syllabus or obtain the textbook to bolster your knowledge of the subject. Preparation programs differ widely in their course offerings, but in general, they should all be based on *Information Power* and should focus on the teaching role of the school library media specialist.

How?

Once you are trying to make the decision of what to do next, you will want to read the section pertaining to score banking and retakes on the NBPTS website. You have several options.

ABANDON THE CANDIDACY

Although you may have trouble reconciling yourself to not completing the process, there may be good reasons why you may decide that you do not want to continue. You may be facing a major family upheaval, such as a new child or a personal or family illness, or you may decide that you want to focus on aspects of life other than this professional growth area. You may think that you tried the certification process, you achieved professional growth, and that alone was worth it.

At some point in your career you may want to repeat the attempt, but if so, you will start over as a first-time candidate.

REPEAT THE ENTIRE ATTEMPT

Each section of the ten-part assessment had a price tag of $350 in 2004 to repeat. The entire process was $2,300, but that rose in 2005 to $2,500. NBPTS permits candidates to repeat as first-time candidates if they choose to do so. This might be a good idea in cases where unforeseen circumstances prevented candidates from giving their best effort uniformly, so that no specific entry was any better or much worse than any other.

If this option is chosen, no score can be banked. The candidate will literally repeat as a first-time candidate.

CHOOSE TO BANK SECTIONS

Most candidates failing to achieve the requisite 2.75 score will choose this option. Candidates will need to consider which entries scored highest, and which entries have the most weight. It also helps to know why certain entries did not score well, and whether the errors and omissions can be easily fixed.

Sections in which the scores were 2.75 or above cannot be banked, which means that candidates cannot choose an area in which they did well and could probably do better in order to raise their overall score.

Choosing which section to redo is not necessarily a difficult choice. Many times, there will be one entry that is very low, and in which the candidate realizes that he or she simply missed the boat completely. Candidates can retake entries twice within two years in order to receive an overall passing score. In some cases, the same entry will present difficulties for some candidates. In these cases, the choice must be made not just to redo, but rather to rethink the entire entry. Something is missing. The candidate must think, discuss, and read to identify the missing pieces.

CAVEATS

It is sometimes helpful to talk about your entry with someone who scored well. Confidentiality rules will prevent you and an NBCT from detailed discussions of an entry or an assessment exercise, but they certainly can tell you what collaborative unit they taught, or how they and their students interacted on their literature entry.

Their advice is valid, but take it with more than a few grains of salt. Remember that the National Board is the only source of valid information about its own certification process. If you are going to talk to candidates, then talk to several of them. When you remove the context from an entry, it removes pretty much the entire set of scorable elements. What worked in one school with one group of students may not work in another. You will have to be careful to glean from talking with other people only the most general areas for improvement.

You may find when you start your investigations that there is something that you truly do not know. The prevailing winds on intellectual freedom may go against your personal religious beliefs. You may firmly believe that denying access to books is perfectly educationally sound for kindergartners, and that they must check out only the books that they can read, and that they can prove to you that they can read.

Collaboration, as reviewed in this book, may be something at which you scoff, knowing that it cannot possibly work in the real world and on a fixed schedule. You may hold the belief that only nonfiction and reference books can be integrated with the curriculum. Fiction books are for fun reading only, and some books are not suitable for any children. You may not do technology, and simply pick up the phone in helpless damsel mode when something doesn't work the way that it should.

When successful candidates talk to you about a library program, you interrupt with reasons why you can't do that in your program. The teachers, parents, students, or administrators will simply not go along with it.

Frankly, in these situations, you may have to admit to yourself that you have a good job, you like it, and everyone thinks that you are good at it. Everyone except the National Board for Professional Teaching Standards. If you are not willing to walk the walk and talk the talk of an accomplished teacher of library media, you simply may not be able to be one.

Can you succeed if you do what you think they want without believing in it? Possibly that could work. The first year that school library media standards were available, there were candidates who did the process while loudly proclaiming that they would be glad to get this process of pretending to be a teacher over with so that they could return to their real job of being a librarian.

Were they successful? Possibly, but it is a dangerous road to tread. But you may end up actually becoming the accomplished National Board Certified Teacher that NBPTS wants you to be anyway. Candidates universally state that applying to be a National Board Certified Teacher is the best professional growth experience they have ever had. You may start out confident that these new processes and new beliefs are hogwash, and that you will return to your tried-and-true ways the minute your portfolio entries are out the door. But something happened along the way, and you found new professional beliefs. That is one outcome of the National Board process.

It is a change process. All change, whether positive or negative, whether it is joy and hope over a new marriage or a new family or grief over a divorce or a death, may have been a difficult change and not one to be eagerly repeated. NBCTs say that they plan instruction differently, that they look at students differently, and that they feel differently about their profession than they did before they went through the process.

NBCT status is like obtaining a driver's license. Whether you are or are not a licensed driver is the point. No one asks how many times you had to take the test. The important part is that you passed.

SUMMARY

NBPTS does not announce the pass rate, but we do know that school library media specialists tend to pass at a higher rate than their classroom teaching peers. Regardless, quite a few library media specialists each year do not pass. It is in the nature of a rigorous process that some people cannot complete the journey.

Although the choice of whether or not to continue is up to each candidate, there is no better way to model persistence for students than to try again. Analyze your entries, reflect on your efforts, then choose your best scores to bank, and try again.

The Future of NBPTS School Library Media Certification

What is the future of National Board certification? We don't truly know at this point. Several states, Maine among them, have discussed automatically certifying teachers who can achieve board certification, with or without appropriate coursework, experience, or training. This has serious ramifications for school library media preparation. Already in some states such as Missouri, passing the PRAXIS exam and spending several years in the position is enough for a clear teaching license in that field. Professionally trained school library media specialists in those states are very concerned about the future of the profession when a test drawn from content knowledge can substitute for years of training in the application of that knowledge.

Allowing NBPTS certification would ensure that competence in teaching the content of library science would be added to the licensure barrier, but there is still concern among those in the field. School library media specialists draw from a wide range of fields to develop their expertise, the two major ones being education and library or information science. The National Board process, regardless of how desirable and how rigorous it may be, does not cover that entire spectrum.

Those coming into the school library field as a midlife career change are primarily from two fields: classroom teaching or from other specialties in library science. Of those groups, it could be possible for strong classroom teachers to achieve NBCT status in school library media with very little training. Those from the library and information sciences would most likely not fare as well. This speaks to a problem in the management of our dual professional background. Teaching is a strong skill set for excellence in school library media, but we cannot leave the library science content area behind.

This debate raged in the 1980s over the best way to educate school library media specialists. As noted in a previous chapter, library educators have spoken eloquently with differing views as to whether school library media specialists should be educator products of library science schools or librarian products of education schools.

School library media specialists have struggled to maintain a professional presence in both the education and the library science fields. It would be foolish to throw away those gains when we have traveled so far. School library media specialists may sometimes feel that they are balanced with one foot on the dock of library and information science and the other on the slowly drifting boat of education. We have struggled to keep our footing for more than a century; this is no time to give up now.

So the impact of the NBPTS process on school library media preparation is largely unknown. The field worries, and rightly so, about whether or not someone who is an experienced teacher of English, social studies, or elementary school might be able to apply those skills to school library media enough to pass the NBPTS process and then become a school library media NBCT. In states accepting the certification, that person would hold a clear licensure, without the full educational process of becoming a professional in the library science and education fields. In other words, without becoming a true school library media specialist.

THE SCHOOL LIBRARY MEDIA SPECIALIST AS NBCT

NBPTS had three goals when it began its work almost twenty years ago. Those goals were to identify the best teachers and create a system of support for them, to change teacher preparation so that more great teachers would be educated, and to make policy changes in the ways that schools were operated. After only three years of interaction, it would be impossible to say whether or not NBPTS will have lasting effects on the school library media profession. However, we can speculate as to the impact it could have.

Identify the Best Teachers

If evidence-based practice and accountability continue to be a factor in education, then those people identified as accomplished teachers will have important skills. Whether or not those skills will be shared and put to use in the field is perhaps something different. AASL has now started a committee and a task force to begin looking at NBCTs as valued professionals. Still, it is evident that only about one quarter to one half of school library media NBCTs are members of their professional association.

Ongoing research by this author is starting to investigate the extent to which the school library media NBCT exemplifies the best practices in the school library media profession. One area found in professional preparation that is an area of concern to most incoming students is how to assess information skills, and then tie that assessment back to schoolwide student accountability standards. The identification of school library media NBCTs may aid in that effort, since the assessment of student learning and other evidence-based practices are key to NBPTS certification.

Change School Library Media Preparation

Change in school library media preparation is already happening to some degree. Most programs, if they are associated with NCATE school library media standards, are already aligned with NBPTS. In the standard program review template, which was used for the first time in spring 2004, programs must provide evidence of candidate performance on specific assessments in order to receive national recognition. Preparation programs must show how they know that candidates for licensure as school library media specialists can collaborate to teach an instructional information skills unit, can deliver a comprehensive reading program, and can integrate technology into instruction.

Those, of course, are the National Board portfolio entries for school library media. With the NCATE template in place, candidates in strong school library preparation programs will receive training in the skills required for the NBPTS process. This should increase the number of NBCTs nationally, which in turn will change how schools view library media specialists as part of the instructional team.

Change the Way That Schools Are Run

More research on the impact of school library media programs is needed before we can show the value of the practices that school library media NBCTs exemplify. As noted in previous chapters, researchers in other classroom teaching fields have already linked high achievement of students to NBCTs in content areas. If we can show that school library media best practices impact students, then we can see the changes that NBCTs bring.

For the first time, we will be able to remove the strength of the resources and structural supports from the lens to see more clearly the behaviors of strong school library media specialists. Research is just beginning in this area, but it looks very promising.

OTHER OPTIONS

It may be that a school library media specialist decides that now is not the right time to apply for National Board certification. Perhaps in five or ten years, or maybe one decides that it is too close to retirement to achieve this level of certification. Involvement in the process is still possible. The assessors for portfolio entries and assessment center exercises must be building-level school library media specialists. There is also a call for more experienced practitioners to act in this role.

Of course, once you are trained as an assessor, you must allow several years to pass before attempting certification yourself. Still, this is a way to learn about the process, and also to be better at what you do on a daily basis. Assessors generally congregate at a city for several weeks in the summer to do the assessments. It's very hard work, but very rewarding as well.

SUMMARY

Certainly NBPTS has the potential to change the field. Our task as a profession is to educate ourselves to see clearly the pendulum that has always swung between our two professions of education and library science. Will NBPTS make each profession stronger, or will we lose sight of our library science roots?

The potential for acceptance of school library media professionals as teaching peers is clear. Unfortunately, there is no equal mechanism for identifying the most accomplished librarians, regardless of specialty. If there were, then school library media specialists could be identified to have the behaviors of excellence we would share with academic, public, and special librarians.

The debate over whether a school library media NBCT is an accomplished teacher of school library media or an accomplished school library media specialist is just beginning, but the answer that may await that discussion may be clearer than we think.

We are both. We are teachers and librarians. We are school library media specialists. Our field, long seen as a generalist specialty in a generalist profession, wears many hats. NBPTS provides the profession with a lens through which to see our teaching role. It is not a new role, but one that may provide a clear vision for the future.

Index

information ethics. *See* Ethics
Information Literacy (assessment center
    exercise 5), 156
Information Power
    administrative tasks, 22, 153
    and ambiguity of library media specialist
        role, 74
    collaboration, 63, 64
    history, 4
    maturity of school library media field, 95
    mission of school library media pro-
        gram, 143
    NBPTS standards visible picture, 30
    pedagogy, 51
    in preparing portfolio, 12
    on users, 24, 78–79
Information Search Process (ISP), 73, 74
information skills processing theory
    in collaboration portfolio entry practice,
        76
    knowledge of, 35
information technology. *See* Technology
inquiry learning, 80
instructional challenges
    in technology integration portfolio entry,
        137–38
instructional collaboration portfolio entry.
    See Collaboration portfolio entry
instructional context section
    collaboration portfolio entry, 114
    literature appreciation portfolio entry,
        127–28
    technology integration portfolio entry,
        137–38
instructional materials
    in literature appreciation portfolio entry,
        130
    in technology integration portfolio entry,
        139–40
instructional methodologies
    and collaboration, 73–74
    in collaboration portfolio entry, 115
    in literature appreciation portfolio entry,
        129
instructional objectives in technology inte-
        gration portfolio entry, 138
integrated instruction. *See also* NBPTS
    Standard 4: Integrating Instruction
    literature activities, 122
    story times, 82
integrated theory and practice, 4–5
Integration of Technology entry. *See*
    Technology integration portfolio entry

intellectual access to library, 43
intellectual freedom
    in assessment center exercises, 153
    in knowledge base, 42, 100–101
interaction in literature appreciation, 123,
    129
International Reading Association, 85
interruptions, handling of, 56
interview as self-assessment technique, 118
I-search information skills methodology, 73,
    74, 156
ISP (Information Search Process), 73, 74

J
Johnson, Doug, 96
journaling
    core principles in, 16
    information technology, 93
    in reflective practice, 59
    and study of standards, 31

K
Kinnell, Susan, 90
Knapp School Library Manpower Project,
    94
knowledge base. *See* Content knowledge
    (knowledge base)
Knowledge of Learners. *See* NBPTS
    Standard 1: Knowledge of Learners
Knowledge of Library and Information
    Studies. *See* NBPTS Standard 3:
    Knowledge of Library and Information
    Studies
Knowledge of Literature (assessment center
    exercise 6), 122, 156–57
Knowledge of Teaching and Learning. *See*
    NBPTS Standard 2: Knowledge of
    Teaching and Learning; Pedagogy
Krashen, Stephen, 83–84, 85
Kuhlthau, Carol, 35, 73, 74, 109, 156

L
Laura Ingalls Wilder awards, 157
leadership in documented accomplishments
    portfolio entry, 143, 145. *See also*
    NBPTS Standard 10: Leadership,
    Advocacy, and Community
    Partnerships
Leading Innovation through the Library
    Media Program. *See* NBPTS Standard
    5: Leading Innovation through the
    Library Media Program

Planning for Instruction section in collaboration portfolio entry, 115
planning in library media center, 35
planning logs, 115
policies and procedures, 92
portfolio entries. *See also specific entries,* *e.g.,* Collaboration portfolio entry
order of completion, 119
process, 11, 50
posters for NBPTS personal space, 45
power relationships and collaboration, 66
PowerPoint presentations, 132, 133
practice for assessment center exercises, 157–58
privacy issues. *See* Right to privacy
problems in work situation in collaboration portfolio entry, 114
professional associations
as core proposition, 10
and professional growth, 142
professional growth. *See also* NBPTS Standard 8: Professional Growth
assistance to others in the community, 42
and documented accomplishments portfolio entry impact on student learning, 141–42, 143, 145
and the university, 4–5
promotion of library
library pan videotape, 131
in literature appreciation portfolio entry, 122, 128
public relations *vs.* advocacy, 95

R

Ranganathan, S. R., 78–79
rapport in collaboration portfolio entry task, 111
reading, encouragement of, 83, 123
reading, teaching of, 83–84
reconsideration of materials. *See* Challenged materials
recruitment and classroom teacher licensure, 22
reference interview, 134
reflective practice. *See also* NBPTS Standard 7: Reflective Practice
as core proposition, 9
on instruction, 52
and professional skills, 41
reflective writing for submissions, 57–59
in collaboration portfolio entry, 111, 116
documented accomplishments portfolio entry, 147–48

literature appreciation portfolio entry, 129–30
and technology integration portfolio entry, 135
in technology integration portfolio entry, 139
research on best practices. *See also* Best practices
access to information, 99–100
advocacy, 96
flexible access, 98–99
literature appreciation, 84–85
research skills. *See* Information literacy
resources
and delivery of instruction, 37
selection of in technology integration portfolio entry, 138
retake candidates. *See* Banking
Riedling, Ann, 74
right to privacy
in standards, 42
in technology integration portfolio entry lesson, 135, 138
risk-taking, modeling of, 50

S

salary increases and NBCTs, 13–14
scaffolding, 139
school library media NBCTs. *See also* NBCTs
demographics, 24–26
future of, 168–70
school library media specialists. *See* Library media specialists
schools, changes in, 169–70
scoring weights, 11, 12
selection criteria for children's literature
and knowledge of resources, 81
story times, 82
written policies for, 101
self-assessment in collaboration portfolio entry, 117–18. *See also* Assessment; Co-assessment
self-censorship, 100–101
separation anxiety, 150
Shannon, Donna, 98
software in assessment center exercises, 155
staff development programs for teachers, 142–43
Standards. *See* NBPTS Library Media Standards; NBPTS Standards
Stripling, Barbara, 35, 73, 75, 109, 156
student achievement and NBCTs, 15

Gail Dickinson has been involved in the National Board for Professional Teaching Standards from the release of the NBPTS Library Media Standards in 2000. She developed and co-hosted a national AASL forum on National Board certification in 2002. She has led several workshops on National Board certification and taught a graduate course at San Jose State University on preparing for National Board certification. Dickinson is currently an assistant professor at the Darden School of Education at Old Dominion University, Norfolk, Virginia.